REA

After hundreds of interviews, visits to the

D
w
co
ha
so

denied boarding compensation. Automobile rental companies keep their best rates a secret when you call for reservations—unless you ask specifically. Credit card companies have great additional benefits, but you have to read the fine print to discover them.

I'm sure this book will help every traveler.

Charlie Leocha

It's well worth waiting for. Some facts may shock even veteran travelers.

Family Travel Times

When asked about passenger bumping rules, excess luggage charges and infant seat policy: "We'd rather you not publish that. We'll be happy to send you a fax on shipping pets."

Northwest Airlines

Internal memo: "Don't kill yourself on this."

"Dave," Public Relations, USAir

Official letter: "Unfortunately, we are too short staffed at this time to provide more customized responses to your questions."

Media Relations Manager, USAir

"In fairness to all, Delta declines participation in projects which require in-depth research such as *Travel Rights*. I'm really sorry we can't help "

Delta Air Lines

"We'll get right back to you."

Continental and TWA

About the Author

Charlie Leocha has been traveling since the age of two when his family moved from Alabama to Virginia. He is an Air Force brat who spent half his life abroad. He had the measles crossing the Atlantic on a troop ship, started school in Naples wearing a smock and bow, sang *If I Had a Hammer* on Red Square in '68, criss-crossed Europe in a camper van, skied at every major resort in America and the Alps, did basic training in the fields of Kansas, rafted in Costa Rica, walked through the rubble of the Berlin Wall, horsebacked through Utah, caroused with flight attendants, and still runs the bulls in Pamplona religiously. He has been stuck in most major U.S. airports, been bumped from scores of flights, and found many ways to be upgraded.

Charlie started a magazine in Europe filled with travel suggestions for Americans living abroad. His *Travel Tips* radio program has been heard on over a hundred stations across the country. He is the creator of the *Escape Manual Travel Guides*, *Skiing America*, *Ski Europe*, and *Eastern Germany*. He has written about travel for dozens of newspapers, and magazines ranging from *Esquire* and *Travel and Leisure* for travelers, to *Travel Agent*, *Business Travel Management* and *Recommend* that serve the travel industry. He knows major airlines from the inside, having led tours, written vacation brochures, produced travel videos and written speeches for airline presidents.

For all of this expertise, he still is heard muttering, while regaling friends about his latest travel adventures, "If only I had known . . ."

TRAVEL RIGHTS

BY CHARLES LEOCHA

WORLD LEISURE CORP.
HAMPSTEAD, NH
BOSTON, MA

© 1994 by Charles A. Leocha

Airline Rights and Effective Complaining
chapters incorporate, update and expand much of
the *Fly Rights* booklet produced by the U.S.
Department of Transportation. Some Fact Boxes
taken from *Guinness Book of World Records
1993*.

Cover design by Tim Gilbert, Orange Slice
Communications, Hampton, NH

Printed in the U. S. A. by Dickinson Press

Distributed to the trade in USA by Login
Publishers Consortium, Chicago, IL 60607;
tel. 312-773-8228

Distributed to the trade in Canada by
General Publishing Co. Ltd., 30 Lesmill Road,
Don Mills, Ontario M3B 2T6, Canada;
tel. 416-445-3333

Distributed to gift stores by Sourcebooks, Inc.
Naperville, IL 60566; tel. 708-961-2161

Distributed to U.S. Military, Stars & Stripes
Bookstores, Mail Order and Special Sales by
World Leisure Corporation, 177 Paris Street,
Boston, MA 02128;
tel. 617-569-1966, fax 617-561-7654

ISBN: 0-915009-28-5

CONTENTS

TRAVEL
RIGHTS

TRAVEL RIGHTS

Share your travel tales

This book will be updated as the world of travel changes, which it surely will. If any of you, our fellow travelers, care to suggest areas we might add to future editions of this book, or juicy stories about travel pitfalls, or tales of exceptional customer service you would like to see practiced by more of the travel industry, please write.

Charlie Leocha
World Leisure Corporation
P.O. Box 160
Hampstead, NH 03841

Disclaimers
Use this book only as a guide.

❑ Most situations can be sorted out with common sense—that is the good part about the limited regulation of the travel industry. Basically, there are few hard and fast rules when it comes to customer service. The company representatives' basic instinct is to keep the customer satisfied, unless you back them into a corner where they may bite back.

❑ Anything we observe in this book, except Federal and international regulations, can be changed without notice, and often is. Nothing is carved in stone—especially when dealing with the travel industry.

❑ We realize that there are many travel situations not covered in this book. We can only scratch the surface of airline, automobile rental, and credit card rights. Hotels have their individual policies, cruise ships each have different regulations, and without doubt tour operators have their own customer service manuals.

❑ Anyone traveling overseas should carefully examine their medical, property and automobile insurance policies to know what situations are and are not covered abroad.

TRAVEL RIGHTS

AN INTRODUCTION TO
YOUR *TRAVEL RIGHTS*

Surprisingly, the travel industry is akin to an Arab souk or Italian street market with lots of room for negotiation before a deal is struck. You probably have had the experience of sitting next to someone who has paid only a fraction of the fare you paid. We all know of people who find the "real deals" when it comes to rental cars. And we have heard of credit card benefits such as rental car Collision Damage Waiver and life insurance, but few of us know the all-important specifics. Getting the best deal is the point of negotiating, but those who don't know the rules won't have a chance.

You may hear flight attendants and airline administrators intone the mantra "Federal Regulation." In actuality, *official* regulation barely exists when it comes to customer service. You have to look behind the regulations to discover the *real* rules by which the travel industry works. We expose some of these rules, and knowing them can make a big, big difference both when planning your trip and when problems arise during your travels.

O If your plane is delayed several hours by a mechanical problem, do airline rules allow you cash, flight vouchers, meals and more?

O If you are bumped off a flight involuntarily and miss a business meeting, do you get the same treatment as a volunteer bumpee, gleeful at the idea of a free ticket?

O Are every airline's rules the same? Absolutely not! One, for example, flies mountain bikes for free, just like skis and ski boots; another charges $45.

O Are charter flights really different from scheduled airlines, or are they only a better bargain?

O When planning to travel with friends and family, and you have *multiple drivers* for a rental car, do you know which companies don't charge extra for additional drivers?

O What credit cards are best for travel? Do you know their real benefits? (One provides *replacement* value insurance for lost baggage.)

O Wonder when you have to pay sales taxes and when you don't? Do you know that after you pay sales taxes in

TRAVEL RIGHTS

Europe *you can get most of your money back*?

○ Do you *really* know how to get a replacement passport in one day when traveling abroad?

This book reveals what your rights are as a passenger and customer of airline, automobile rental, and credit card companies. In actuality, legal rights are few, but since these companies compete aggressively, they each operate according to a well-defined individual company code, their Passenger Service Manual, which gives their service relative consistency.

These following pages are packed with eye-opening discriptions of airline and rental car rules and regulations, which together with federal and international regulations create the semi-legal tangle all passengers must negotiate. Even travel veterans and tested road warriors will be surprised at many airline services, Big Brother links between rental car companies and DMVs, and the significant but unsuspected benefits you carry in your pocket with many credit cards.

Once upon a time getting Point A to Point B was a rather straightforward proposition —you negotiated with the camel caravan master or the clipper ship agent and then took your chances. You paid to reach a

TRAVEL RIGHTS

destination: *when* you arrived (and your condition when you got there) were not part of the bargain. This is no longer true.

Today, the Zen of Travel predominates, and reaching your destination is no longer the ultimate goal. The journey there, with some sense of style and comfort, is more important. Airlines rarely compete based on destination but instead on size of seats, frequency of service, and on-time records. Rental car companies no longer seem to be in the business of renting cars—their advertising shows customers floating through airports for no-wait service.

The bottom line is that travelers need to know what their options may be. For an airline or rental car company to keep its policies operationally secret, so as to provide the customer with the least possible compensation for delays or difficulties, is absurd. We hope this book sheds a bit of light on the world we travel in, and helps with everyday travel negotiations.

Charles Leocha

AIRLINE

RIGHTS

The airline industry seems at first glance to be one of the most regulated sectors of the world economy, with aviation authorities and commissions abounding everywhere on the globe. Air traffic is closely monitored, aircraft are carefully inspected and expertly maintained, routes are approved by bureaucracies, small regional carriers are subsidized, reservation systems are scrutinized, flight records are kept mile by mile, and much more.

Though you seem to hear "due to Federal regulation" after every sentence when your flight attendant gives a safety briefing, in the area of passenger service the industry is barely regulated. The Department of Transportation (DOT) has established a barebones Code of Federal Regulation and each air carrier designs its own rules to fall within these limits. During the research of this book, DOT was more helpful and responsive than I previously believed a government bureaucracy could be.

Unfortunately, few carriers want you to know what their specific rules are. Of the U.S.-owned airlines, United Airlines was clearly the most helpful in providing materials for our research. American Airlines also responded quickly and answered most of our questions. As for the others, it seems that an educated passenger is not exactly an airline's dream customer. Rather than clearly outline their passenger handling procedures, the airlines would much rather have consumers who accept what they are told and ask for nothing more.

Even when I called, faxed and wrote, many airlines such as USAir protested that they were "too short-staffed to provide more customized answers" to my questions. Northwest simply stated that they would rather we didn't publish any of the information requested. They then acquiesced and sent a fax on shipping pets. Delta wrote that they "declined to participate in projects such as *Travel Rights*." TWA and Continental kept their heads stuck in the sand and never responded.

All airlines aggressively guard their passenger service manuals as proprietary information with excuses such as "they change too frequently for external use"—an amazing response when you consider they can implement fare changes with the speed and frequency of rabbits mating, and spend millions of dollars to tell the public what they want it to know.

These internal rules and regulations are part of each airline's competitive posture within the industry. The level of service provided to passengers by airlines is now as important a consideration for most travelers as finding a nonstop flight and securing the lowest airfare. As you use this book, realize that we provide only *guidelines* for your fly rights—every airline has its own domestic and international rules.

NEGOTIATING THROUGH THE AIRFARE MAZE

Because of deregulation and the resulting emphasis on price competition, airlines don't all charge the same fares anymore. Some of them are trying a "back to basics" approach—offering plane rides at bargain basement prices with few if any such extras as meals and baggage transfer.

Most airlines have more than a dozen different types of fares for domestic flights and as many as 75 in various international markets. But there are some basic fare groups that serve as a starting point for breaking them down.

The rule these days is to compare. Never accept the first fare quoted. Many times, another flight on another airline within an hour of the time you want to fly will provide a less expensive deal.

The three classes offer the principal breakdown of fares and are operated as separately as possible from each other.

✈ **First Class** is the top-of-the-line service with wide seats (some that fully recline), sometimes beds, and meals far too extensive and rich for any normal traveler to consume, served on fine china with silverware, all accompanied by flasks of vintage wine and champagne as well as port, cognac and liqueurs.

✈ **Business Class** is normally a significant step below First Class. Here seats are not as large nor do they recline as far, you won't find beds, and the wines and spirits are far more pedestrian. (Some airlines are now eliminating First Class and replacing it with a souped-up Business Class)

✈ **Coach Class** is the back of the plane. Here seats are narrow with only minimal reclining possibilities. Meals on most airlines are served on plastic and consumed with similar utensils. On U.S. carriers, you usually pay for any beverage other than basic juices, carbonated sodas and water. Even offering exorbitant sums won't improve the wine selection. On foreign airlines a bottle of wine or beer is often included in Coach Class price.

Within each of these classes there are many fare variations. At this point the important fact to remember is that the fares you would pay—if you merely walked up to the counter and purchased a ticket for a flight on that same day—are nothing short of mind-bogglingly high. **So you have to plan ahead.**

With planning you can take advantage of tickets such as:

- ✈ 14-day advance purchase
- ✈ 7-day advance purchase
- ✈ round-trip Saturday-night stayover
- ✈ deep-discount tickets (often called supersavers)
- ✈ and more . . .

For the information you need to negotiate this pricing maze, you can contact a travel agent, an airline serving the places you want to visit, or a consolidator (see page 25). With a little research in local papers, by telephone or on computer services, you can find all airlines flying to your destination. Then you can call each airline to ask about their fares and any special deals they may offer. You can also watch the newspapers where airlines advertise many of their most heavily discounted plans. Finally, be alert to new companies serving the market. They may offer lower fares than older established airlines.

Here are some tips to help you decide between airfares:

- ● Be flexible in your travel plans if you want the lowest fare. Often there are complicated conditions you must meet to qualify for a discount. The most usual requirement is that you purchase your ticket at least 14 days in advance (sometimes seven days in advance, sometimes less) and stay over a Saturday night.

● Plan as far ahead as you can. Some airlines set aside only a few seats on each flight at the low rates, so that the real bargains often sell out very quickly. (But you can keep trying— the airline may change its number of deep-discount seats several times during any promotion.)

● Some airlines may have discounts that others don't offer. In a large metropolitan area, the fare could depend on which airport you use.

● Does the airfare include types of service that airlines have tradition- ally provided, such as meals or free baggage handling? (Many of the low-fare scheduled airlines only serve snacks and soda, and they nor- mally do not participate in what is called interlining of baggage—the transfer of bags between airlines.)

● If you are stranded, will the ticket be good on another airline at no extra charge? Will the first airline pay for meals or hotel rooms?

● Find out what will happen if you decide to switch flights. Will you lose the benefit of your discount fare? Are there any cancellation fees? Is there a cutoff date for making and changing reservations without paying more money?

● Some airlines will not increase the fare after the ticket is issued and paid for. (*However*: merely holding a reservation without a ticket does not guarantee the fare.) Before you buy your ticket, ask if the fare can be increased later.

● Remember, when you purchase a non-refundable ticket, the ticket is what the name implies—non-refundable, even only two hours later (unless you use a travel agent—see next section). Most airlines, however, will allow you to apply the cost of the ticket to another ticket on their airline.

● Differences in airfare can be substantial. Careful comparison shopping between airlines does take time, but it can lead to real savings.

Rules that apply to charter flights are covered starting on page 73.

TRAVEL
RIGHTS

Those over the age of 62 have one of the best bargains in the airline industry with their senior coupons. Though the coupon airfares are not always lower than super-saver fares for short hauls, they are convenient and easy to use. Also, many airlines add a 10 percent senior discount to even the deepest discount ticket. For long-haul tickets there are few better deals.

☛ Some senior coupon highlights:

● Some airlines allow companions (any age) of seniors to fly with a senior coupon. At press time, Air Canada and TWA had this liberal policy. USAir limits these companions to ages 2 to 11.

● In Canada you only have to be 60 to qualify for senior coupons.

● Most senior coupons give frequent-flier credit, except TWA.

● If you need a wheelchair or agent assistance, make your request at the same time as your reservation. Check again when you arrive at the airport and have airline personnel call ahead to your destination or connection.

Bereavement fares

These fares are for people who must travel to a funeral or immediately visit a sick relative. There are no firm and fast rules for these fares in the industry, but they are definitely back after being sacrificed temporarily on the altar of fare simplification.

These fares are normally not as inexpensive as supersaver fares or advance-purchase coach fares, but they are much less expensive than the normal business traveler fares.

> Be sure to be able to document your bereavement or emergency.

Some airlines require that you pay full fare, but state that you will receive a partial rebate after the trip. Find out if the rebate is in cash or merely in the form of vouchers for future travel on that carrier.

Since the formula for bereavement fares varies so much from airline to airline, you should check the rates of all airlines that offer service to your destination and find out what documentation, if any, is required to secure the bereavement fare.

Child fares

Passengers who have reached their second birthday are expected to pay the applicable adult fare.

✔ As noted above, on some airlines senior citizens with senior coupons (meaning Grandma or Grandpa for the most part) with a child under the age of 11 can also use a senior coupon for the child's fare.

Internationally there is a bit more of a break on ticket prices, with children 2 to 11 paying 50 to 75 percent of the applicable fare.

In Europe there are Youth Fares available which offer semi-standby travel for youths aged 12 to 24. These seats normally are only confirmed within 72 hours of departure for both legs of a trip, so they offer plenty of flexibility.

Unaccompanied minors

Even though the charges are the same for minors and adults, the rights to travel are not. On most airlines, unaccompanied children under the age of 5 are not allowed.

Unaccompanied minors 5 to 7 years of age may be accepted on a nonstop or through flight and must be accompanied by a responsible adult until the child is boarded. The child must be met by a responsible adult.

Unaccompanied children 8 through 11 years of age may be accepted on nonstop, through or connecting flights. Reservations must be confirmed to the destination. Children making connections will be assisted by the airline (if your child is changing *airlines*, make sure airline personnel will "hand off" your child to the next carrier—most won't, so plan on a single airline flight). The child must be accompanied by a responsible adult until the child is boarded. The child must be met by a responsible adult.

Unaccompanied children 12 through 17 years of age may receive assistance making connecting flights upon request.

Most airlines charge an additional fee of $25 to $30 to escort a child onto another plane when making connections.

If you are sending a young child on an airline journey alone, check the airline policy.

✔ Tips for parents sending their children on a flight:

● Try to make the reservations on a nonstop or direct flight. In some cases this is required.

● Introduce your child to the gate agent and REMIND the agent that your child will need assistance changing planes when appropriate.

TRAVEL
RIGHTS

- Let the cabin crew know if this is the child's first flight—they will do their best to reassure the child.

- Do not book your child on the last flight of the evening. In the event of a delay or missed connection the child will have to spend the night alone in a strange city.

- Tuck in a pocket or in a pouch around the child's neck all identification information, with the child's name and destination, the flight numbers and schedule, your name, your address, your phone number, and whether any luggage was checked. (The Travel Card on the next pages provides a good outline of information.)

- Remember to give the child some spending money for movie headsets, phone calls, or food in case of a delay. Let them know what is free and what they have to pay for.

- Try to get a window seat.

- Give your child games and books to help keep occupied during the flight.

- Order a child's meal 4 to 24 hours in advance, depending on the airline.

- Let children know who will be picking them up at the airport when they arrive.

- Tell the person picking up your child on the other end of the flight to bring proper identification. No airline will release a child without it. Children will only be released to adults listed on a travel card or the Unaccompanied Minor Forms, provided by the airline.

- Call ahead to let the folks meeting the flight know what time the plane actually took off.

> **TWYCH—Travel With Your Children,** based in New York, publishes an excellent detailed *Airline Guide* for children's travel details on most major airlines, for both accompanied and unaccompanied children.
>
> Subscribers to *Family Travel Times* get one free; non-subscribers may purchase a copy of the latest edition for $10 plus $2 postage and handling by sending a check to: TWYCH, 45 W. 18th St., 7th Floor, New York, NY 10011.

TRAVEL CARD

SEAT # _____

Name of child: _____
Age: _____

Name of sender: _____

Address: _____

Telephone: Day _____

        Evening _____

Name of Receiver: _____

Address: _____

Telephone: Day _____

        Evening _____

Airline Information

Airline:_____Flight #_____
Destination_____Ticket #_____
Departure Time _____Arrival Time_____

List of connecting flights
Airline_____Flight #_____
Destination _____Ticket #_____
Departure Time _____Arrival Time_____

Airline:_____Flight #_____
Destination_____Ticket #_____
Departure Time_____Arrival Time_____

Passport # _____

(for international travel)

If necessary attach Medical Alert

**TRAVEL
RIGHTS**
15

Infants and infant seats

Infant seats are now recommended, *not required*, by the Federal Aviation Administration, but in most cases, you'll have to pay full fare for the seat your child occupies to reserve and guarantee a place.

If the infant seat is not FAA-approved, some airlines will not allow you to bring it aboard—you may wish to ask the airline for a list of approved infant seats. However, with the exception of homemade car seats or baby feeder seats, almost every car seat manufactured today meets FAA standards. Call the FAA (see p. 137) for their booklet, *Child/Infant Safety Seats Recommended for Use in Aircraft*.

There are several options for avoiding the purchase of an extra ticket for an infant:

● Hold the child on your lap during the flight. If you do this, children under the age of 2 can fly free domestically and for 10 percent of full adult fare internationally. One "carry-on" child is allowed per adult.

● NOTE: The 10 percent you pay for an infant on an international flight does not pay for a guaranteed seat—you still are expected to hold the child on your lap should the flight be full.

- Some parents prefer a bulkhead seat with a bassinet. The bassinet can be used after takeoff for small infants, but you still must hold the infant on your lap for takeoff and landing. Make your request for a bassinet early. Some airlines are more helpful with bassinets than others. Ask other parents about their experiences.

- Many parents feel bulkhead seats are undesirable since there is no under-seat storage, the armrests don't fold up and down, and some don't have tables. Unless you are using a bassinet another seat may be best.

- Bring your own infant seat with you on the plane and hope for an empty seat next to you. Most airlines will allow you to use the infant seat on a space-available basis.

- Purchase an infant ticket. At press time most major airlines had no infant fare; however, that may change in the near future—ask. (Southwest; Airlines was the only carrier with an infant fare—about 60 percent of the adult fare—that will guarantee a seat.)

- Most major airlines *will reserve the seat next to you* if you are traveling with an infant. That seat will only be used if the flight is full.

- Bring your own infant food or ask the airline specifically whether baby-food meals are available. Call at least 24 hours in advance.

Money-saving tactics

✔ Airlines, after a lot of vocal opposition, now tacitly allow the "nesting" of airfares. Nesting is a way around what is called the Saturday-night rule. Deep-discounted tickets provide significant savings, but they require that the airline passenger stay over a Saturday night. This was to discourage high-fare business travelers from buying low-fare leisure-travel tickets: the Saturday-night rule meant the businessmen either had to stay away from their families over the weekends or fork over higher fares.

Provided you are traveling to the same destination at least twice within the same fare period, nesting will allow you to purchase one round-trip ticket from your home and a second round-trip ticket from your destination and nest them to circumvent the Saturday-night rule.

You need at least two round-trip tickets to nest. Example:

1. Fly Boston to Dallas Monday morning with your first round-trip ticket.
2. Return to Boston Friday with the second round-trip ticket.
3. The following Monday, leave again for Dallas using the return portion of your second round-trip ticket.
4. Return to Boston on Friday with the return portion of your first ticket.

Airlines don't like this, but they now have agreed to accept these fare-saving arrangements.

✔ Examine or have your travel agent carefully examine discount supersaver airfares if you are planning a trip seven to 14 days in advance, but can't stay over a Saturday night. You will often find that it is less expensive to purchase two separate round-trip supersaver tickets, discarding the *return* portions of each, rather than buy a standard coach round trip.

FREQUENT FLIER NOTE:
Remember that normally your frequent flier benefits are considered part of your estate. Most award mileage will be transferred to the heir's account or handled according to the will. Once again, the rules vary between airline frequent flier programs, but most programs have a way of dealing with accrued mileage as an asset of an estate.

AIRLINE TICKET CONTRACT TERMS

There is a written contract between you and an airline created every time you purchase a ticket. It is important to realize, however, that each airline has specific rules that make up what is called your contract of carriage. Your contract of carriage is not necessarily your ticket. The difference is explained below. These rules may differ between carriers. They include provisions such as check-in deadlines, limits on liability for lost baggage, responsibility for delayed flights, and many other things.

Airlines are required to show passengers these complete terms in writing if they ask. Note: Contract Terms for "Express" divisions of airlines, such as United Express (in effect independent regional airlines), are different from the parent airline.

Domestic travel

For domestic travel, some airlines provide all contract terms on or with your ticket at the time you buy it. Many small commuter carriers use this system. Other airlines may elect to "incorporate terms by reference" into their contracts of carriage for domestic transportation. This means that you are not given all the airline's rules with your ticket—most of them are contained in a separate document that you can inspect on request.

If an airline elects to incorporate by reference it must provide conspicuous written notice with each ticket that:

l) it incorporates terms by reference, and

2) these terms may include liability limitations, claim-filing deadlines, check-in deadlines, and certain other key terms; the airline must also:

- Ensure that passengers can receive an explanation of key terms identified on the ticket from any location where the carrier's tickets are sold, including travel agencies;

- Make available for inspection the full text of its contract of carriage at each of its own airport and city ticket offices; and

- Mail a free copy of the full contract of carriage upon written request.

There are additional notice requirements for contract terms that affect your airfare. Airlines must provide a conspicuous written notice on or with the ticket concerning any "incorporated" contract terms that:

- Restrict refunds;
- Impose monetary penalties; or

● Permit the airline to raise the price after you've bought the ticket.

If a U.S. airline incorporates contract terms by reference and fails to provide the required notice about a particular rule, the passenger will not be bound by that rule.

International travel

The detailed requirements for disclosing domestic contract terms do not apply to international travel. Airlines file Tariff Rules with the government for international service. Passengers are generally bound by these rules whether or not they receive actual notice of them.

Every international airline must keep a copy of its tariff rules at its airport and city ticket offices. You have a right to examine these rules. The airline agents must answer your questions about information in the tariff, and they must help you locate specific tariff rules, if necessary.

The most important point to remember, whether your travel is domestic or international, is that you should not be afraid to ask questions about an airline's rules. You have a right to know the terms of your contract of carriage. It is in your best interest, as well as the airline's, for you to ask in advance about any matters of uncertainty.

TRAVEL AGENTS & CONSOLIDATORS

Why a travel agent can help

Travel agents sell most of the airline tickets and hotel rooms in America. Hence, a travel agent often has clout and know-how that can make your trip easier and more enjoyable. **NOTE:** All travel agents are not the same. Some specialize in European travel, others are experts in Asian travel, others deal with cruise ships, and yet others provide bargain-basement travel throughout the year. However, the following points apply to all of them:

● Your airfare is the same whether you purchase your tickets directly from the airline or through a travel agent.

● With airfares changing as quickly as they seem to, travel agents provide the easiest way to change tickets in order to get a lower airfare if one should be implemented between the time you purchase your ticket and your flight. There are no advantages to buying your tickets directly from the airlines. Though airlines claim they can reissue your tickets at the new lower rates, you have to go to the airport, or an airline ticket office, which in most cases is less convenient than using your local travel agent.

● If you purchase your ticket through a travel agent you have more leeway for payment, since agencies normally make their payments to the airlines once a week. If you work frequently with an agent they will let you know their payment day, normally Tuesday at noon. They may sometimes cancel a ticket if you change your mind within a day or so. They can also place last-minute reservations before special fares expire and then bill you for the ticket, giving you about a week before you actually have to pay.

● If there is a problem, your travel agent is probably a member of the American Society of Travel Agents, which has an excellent consumer protection program (see page 139).

What is a consolidator?

A consolidator is a discount airline ticket seller. Most of these operations are closely aligned with the major airlines. When normal airline deep-discounts still leave significant numbers of empty seats available on a given flight, the airlines release seats to consolidators who can sell these discounted tickets through travel agents or in some cases directly to the public. You might call them the "factory outlets" of airlines. As with many discount stores, the names of the airlines are not advertised. You will be told of your airline choices before you purchase any tickets, and they will be clearly marked on your ticket.

Consolidator fares normally are competitive with advance-purchase airfares; *however:* you do not have to purchase your ticket until the day of the flight if seats are still available. Your benefit is flexibility of purchase time, combined with advance-purchase pricing. NOTE: Consolidator tickets may be more expensive than deep-discount promotions. Make sure to do your homework.

✔ **Consolidators have several drawbacks:**

● Depending on the type of ticket you purchase, you may not be eligible for frequent-flier mileage credits or frequent-flier upgrades.

● Your choice of airline and selection of available flight times are also limited. Also, with many consolidator tickets you may only get seat assignments at flight time at the airport, and some of these tickets also preclude special meals (See page 35).

- Your ticket theoretically is only valid on the airline originally indicated on the ticket. If there is a flight cancellation or delay you will either have to take a later flight on that airline, which may mean staying overnight, or purchase a full-fare ticket, eliminating any discount benefit. (Reportedly, some airlines have been known to make unofficial arrangements for stranded consolidator ticket holders, but don't bet on it.)

- Consolidator tickets cannot be refunded through the airlines—they must be refunded through the consolidator. In some cases they are non-refundable. Purchase consolidator tickets only with a credit card. If the consolidator goes bankruptcy or fails to send you your ticket, you can cancel the charge.

For more information on consolidators, ask your travel agent. They normally work with several consolidators for international and domestic travel. The *Consumer Reports Travel Letter* often reports on international and domestic airline consolidators and has back issues available.

▲ **NOTE:** Currently, most non-refundable tickets purchased from airlines can be reapplied to another flight upon payment of a small fee if your plans change; consolidators may not allow that flexibility.

RESERVATIONS
AND TICKETS

Once you decide when and where you want to go, and which airline you want to use, getting reservations and tickets is a fairly simple process. You can make all your arrangements by telephone, at the airline's ticket office, or through a travel agent or other ticket marketer. There are a few potential pitfalls, however, and these pointers should help you avoid them.

● If your travel falls into a busy period, call for reservations early. Flights for holidays may sell out weeks—sometimes months—ahead of time.

● When you make a reservation, be sure the airline records the information accurately. Before you hang up or leave the ticket office, review all of the essential information with the agent—the spelling of your name, the flight numbers and travel dates, and the cities you are traveling between. If there is more than one airport at either city, be sure to check which one you'll be using. It's also important to give the airline your home and work telephone numbers so that they can let you know about any changes in the schedule.

- Whenever you call an airline to make reservations or purchase a ticket, get the reservation or confirmation number. This number makes it much easier to settle any future question that may arise about your reservation.

- Your ticket will show the flight numbers, departure times and dates, and status of your reservations for each leg of your itinerary. The "status" box is important. "OK" means you're confirmed. Anything else means you're only wait-listed or that the reservation is not yet certain.

- When an agent says you must buy your tickets by a specific time or date, this is a deadline. If you don't purchase your ticket before the deadline, the airline may cancel your reservations without further notification.

- If your reservations are booked far enough ahead of time, the airline may offer to mail your tickets. Otherwise, check the telephone directory for the nearest ticket office or travel agency and buy your tickets there.

- Try to have your tickets in hand before you go to the airport. This is smart traveling. It helps avoid some of the tension you may otherwise feel if you

TRAVEL RIGHTS

have to wait in a slow-moving ticket line and worry about missing your flight.

Reconfirming flights

✔ It's a good idea to reconfirm your reservations before each flight on your trip; flight schedules sometimes change. On international trips, most airlines require that you reconfirm your onward or return reservations at least 72 hours before each flight. If you don't, your reservations may be canceled. We recommend that every international traveler always reconfirm, since some airlines are much more rigid on this requirement than others.

> Don't be a "no-show." If you are holding confirmed reservations you don't plan to use, notify the airline as soon as you're definite about not taking that flight.

Airline seat reservations Advance seat selection and boarding passes

A relatively recent change in reservation operations is the ability to make your seat selection well before your flight. Each airline has its own time limit: some permit selection as long as 90 days in advance and others not until 30 days before your scheduled flight.

✔ Getting to the airport early used to guarantee getting a good seat. Today, with advance seat selection, this is no longer the case. In fact, advance selection is important for the reasons noted below.

● The most obvious reason is to avoid sitting in the uncomfortable middle seat of a three-seat row. If you make your selection early you can normally get a window or aisle seat. At the gate this may be impossible.

● If you are traveling with a partner the best strategy to insure an empty seat next to you is for one of you to reserve the window seat and the other the aisle seat of the same row, toward the rear of the aircraft. This leaves the middle seat unreserved and these seats (especially those in the rear center rows) tend to be the last assigned.

● If you are traveling alone, ask the reservations agent to assign you a window or aisle seat in a row where another single is already assigned a window or aisle seat.

● On wide-body aircraft, the center section is the last to fill up. If you ask for an aisle seat in the center section you will have the best chance of having an empty seat beside you.

TRAVEL RIGHTS

● In case of an overbooked flight, anyone without a preassigned seat is treated virtually as a standby passenger. You will often have to wait until the last minute to board and are at the mercy of no-shows for available seats.

> **NOTE:** Even if you have an advance boarding pass, it doesn't mean you can wander onto the plane only minutes before the flight. You must *still* let the airline personnel know you have arrived at the airport, so as not to be bumped or lose your reserved seat.

✔ Other seating considerations:

● If you do not like your preassigned seat, ask for a window, aisle or bulkhead seat when you check in at the airport. The airlines often do not release certain seats, such as bulkhead seats, until the day of the flight. If the ticket agent cannot help you, ask again at the gate. Gate personnel have much more immediate control of seating.

● If you have an uncomfortable preassigned seat, check with airline personnel at the boarding gate. They will release any unclaimed seats about 10 minutes before the flight and you normally can be reassigned an aisle or window seat.

● If you are already on the plane stuck in the middle seat or cramped next to an obese passenger, check out the airplane for any better empty seats. As soon as the passenger door closes, you may move to the better seat (in the same class of service) for a much more enjoyable flight. If you are on the first leg of a direct flight, you may have to move at the intermediate city. The seat may be assigned to a passenger boarding there.

● The safest seats on most aircraft are in the back third of the aircraft. According to articles based on recent published studies, the rear of the plane is up to 34 percent safer than the front, with the exception of some 727s with their rear air-stair exits.

● Exit rows are often roomier, but normally aren't released until the day of the flight; children under 15 are restricted from these seats. These seats also have additional restrictions which basically require that you can see and hear adequately and are physically able to open the emergency exits. (Exit row seats are also generally colder.)

- Avoid seats just in front of emergency exits—they do not recline much, if at all, so as to keep the exit clear in case of an emergency.

- Choose the aircraft you will be flying if possible. 727s, 737s and 757s are the most cramped. 767s, Airbuses and MD-80s are among the most comfortable. Some airlines offer greater pitch (distance between seats)—check with travel agents and friends or read *Consumer Report Travel Letter* for a list of the roomiest airlines.

- Bulkhead seats sometimes have extra legroom and always eliminate the possibility of someone reclining their seat into your face. The tradeoff may be a poor view of the movie, no permanent tray, and no storage area under the seat in front of you (everything has to go in overhead storage).

- Charter DC10s, L1011s and newer MD11s with 10-across seating are the worst. Avoid them if you can.

- If you are a non-smoker, remember that most international flights have smoking sections. You'll want to make sure you are not in the last rows of the non-smoking area, subjected to second-hand smoke floating into your section.

Special meals

✔ In addition to selecting seats, travelers can select special meals on many airlines. Last year, United Airlines, for example, served over 2 million special meals (6,000 per day). These must be ordered six to 24 hours, depending on the airline, before your flight departure. Any unforeseen change in your schedule will nullify your meal request. (Note: Special meals are not available on all flights or for all fares.)

☛ KLM Royal Dutch Airlines offers 13 special meals in four categories—Diet, Religious, Vegetarian, and Children's. Their special meal selections include:
• Diabetic • Low cholesterol/low fat • Low calorie • Low sodium • High fiber • Kosher • Moslem • Hindu • Western vegetarian • Strict vegetarian • Asian vegetarian • Baby food and Child meals.

☛ Other airlines offer Gluten-free (no wheat, rye, barley, or oats), Bland (no seasoning), High protein, Lacto-vegetarian, Fruit, Seafood, Oriental, Kosher, Hamburgers, Peanut butter and jelly sandwiches, and sometimes even a birthday or wedding cake. United Airlines even offers Obento (a chilled Japanese meal) and McDonald's Friendly Skies Meals for children on some flights. USAir has chicken legs and tater tots. Delta serves pizza.

PAYMENTS & REFUNDS ON AIRLINE TICKETS

- If you plan to pay in person and with your own bank check, take along least two forms of identification such as a driver's license, major credit card, and employee ID card. Airlines, travel agencies and other ticket sellers will want to confirm your identity, particularly when you purchase tickets far from your home town.

- If you pay for your ticket with cash or personal check, the ticket refund will generally have to be processed through the airline accounting department and mailed to you. The airlines have 20 business days—a calendar month—to process your refund.

- When you pay by credit card, your account is billed, whether you use your tickets or not. You won't receive credit unless the unused tickets are returned to the airline or travel agency, and you can't get a cash refund for a credit card charge. The credit card refund, however, is immediate.

- If you buy your ticket with a credit card and then change your flight, the ticket agent may want to credit the amount of the old ticket and issue another with a second charge to your account. You can insist that the value of your old tickets be applied to the new ones, with the difference in price charged or credited to your account. While this creates a little extra work for the airlines, it prevents double-billing on your card.

- If you pay by credit card and have trouble getting a refund for a refundable ticket, report this *in writing* to your credit card company. If you write them within 60 days after they mailed your statement showing the charge for the ticket, they should credit your account.

- If the airline goes bankrupt, you can get a refund on your credit card. If you paid by cash or by check, there may be a very long and unfruitful wait.

- Most airline tickets are good for one year—after that time it may be difficult or impossible to get a refund.

If you don't use an airline ticket for its original flight, you can usually change it. Most airlines will apply the fare printed on the ticket to another flight or itinerary. Because of this ease of exchange, your ticket is like currency: if you lose it, anyone who picks it up can take it to any airline and exchange it for transportation on a different flight—even to another city. Replacing or refunding a lost ticket can be a major nuisance.

As a precaution, jot down the ticket number on a separate sheet of paper. Better, photocopy the ticket and put the copy in a place where you're not likely to lose it, or give it to a friend. If your ticket is lost, the airline can process your refund application more quickly, and perhaps issue an on-the-spot replacement, with this information.

✔ Report a lost ticket immediately to the *airline* that issued the ticket. (If you bought the ticket from a travel agent or other outlet, the issuing airline is the one whose name was imprinted on the ticket.)

Once the airline establishes that you actually bought the ticket, they will process your refund application. Some airlines will do this right away, while others may wait up to six months. If anyone uses or cashes in your ticket while the refund is pending, the airline may refuse to give you your money back. Finally, there is a handling charge ($35-$50) that the airline may deduct from the refund.

All in all, getting a refund or replacement for a lost ticket is a lot of trouble, and there's no guarantee you'll receive either. So the best advice is—don't lose the ticket in the first place.

DELAYED &
CANCELED FLIGHTS

Airlines don't guarantee their schedules, and you should realize this when planning your trip. There are many things that can, and often do, make it impossible for flights to leave on time. Some of these problems, like bad weather, air traffic delays, and mechanical repairs, are hard to predict and beyond the airlines' control.

This is an area that is not controlled by any laws. Each airline has its own policies.

If your flight is delayed, try to find out why. But keep in mind that the airline employees may not have the answer. If the problem is with local weather or air traffic control, all flights will probably be late and there's not much you or the airline can do to speed up your departure. If there's a mechanical problem with your plane, or if the crew is delayed on an incoming flight, you might be better off trying to arrange a flight on another airline, as long as you don't have to pay a cancellation penalty or higher fare for changing your reservations. Ask the first airline to "endorse" (authorize the transfer of) your ticket to the new carrier; this could save you a fare increase.

If the flight is canceled, some airlines will rebook you at no additional charge on the first flight to your destination on which space is available. Finding space may be difficult, however, at holidays and peak travel times. Many airlines, if the cancellation was caused by other than an Act of God, will compensate you with a coupon for a free flight, similar to denied boarding compensation (see page 46), if you ask.

✔ **NOTE**: Rather than wait in a long line at the ticket counter or boarding gate for a seat reservation after an unexpected flight cancellation, call the toll-free reservations number and ask the agent to book you on the next available flight. That way you immediately lock in a new flight. You will only have to wait in line for the ticket change, but with great peace of mind.

Each airline has its own policies about what it will do for delayed passengers waiting at the airport. If you are delayed, check with the airline staff to find out what services they will provide. Ask about meals and phone calls. Basically, if the delay is mechanical (the airline's fault) and for more than an hour they will go overboard to help; if the delay is due to weather (Act of God) you're on your own.

Though the airlines will all vehemently deny it, passengers traveling with a full-fare coach ticket or full-fare Business Class or First Class will have more clout and often receive better compensation. Some of this treatment, such as easy endorsements to other airlines, is built into the fare structure. Sometimes the treatment, such as a free flight coupon or entry into the airline clubs, is based on the airline's interest in keeping a full-fare-paying passenger.

Some airlines, often those charging very low fares, do not provide any amenities to stranded passengers. Others may not offer amenities if the delay is caused by something beyond the airline's control.

Airlines almost always refuse to pay passengers for financial losses resulting from a delayed arrival. If the purpose of your trip is to close a lucrative business deal, to give a speech or lecture, to attend a family function, or to be present at any other time-sensitive event, you may want to allow a little extra leeway and take an earlier flight. In other words, airline delays and cancellations aren't unusual, and defensive counterplanning is a good idea when time is your most important consideration.

If you are holding a full-fare ticket, or any ticket for that matter, and you don't want to add to the confusion at the airport, but feel you should receive *some* compensation for a delay within the airline's control, write a letter to the airline's Customer Service Office. The addresses and phone numbers are listed in the back of this book.

✔ Suggestions for anyone running late for a connection:

● If your flight is late and your connection at the next airport is in jeopardy, tell a flight attendant while you are in flight or let the gate agent know if you are still at the gate. Some airlines will make arrangements to take you by car or van between terminals, or use small electric carts that can get to your gate much faster than you can walk. If there are enough late connecting passengers, airlines may delay connecting flights.

● While on the airplane check the in-flight magazine for a diagram of the airport where you will be landing. The flight attendant can find out your arrival gate and that of your connecting flight. Knowing the layout of the airport can help you move a bit faster.

● As soon as you get off the plane let a customer service agent know about your problem. They often have radios or cellular phones and will call ahead to the gate to let the boarding personnel know you are on your way. The boarding crew also are in contact with the electric carts scooting between gates.

✔ Suggestions for anyone dealing with a predicted snowstorm or severe weather:

● If your flight turns out to be scheduled on the same day as a predicted snowstorm

TRAVEL RIGHTS

or other major weather problem, check with your airline to find out whether or not you can attempt to fly out on standby status the day *before* the snowstorm. Even if the telephone agent can't give you an answer, head to the airport. You'll find that, normally, most airline airport personnel are happy to get as many passengers out of their hair before the predicted cancellations and delays. I learned from one airline, operating from Boston before a predicted one-foot snowstorm, that all penalties and charges for changing all categories of tickets had been suspended for three days in order to ease the crunch at the airport during the storm.

✔ Suggestions for anyone changing a non-refundable or special-fare ticket:

● Airlines often will allow you to change your ticket from one local airport to another without a charge. For instance, you may decide that it would be easier to fly from JFK rather than Newark. Make these changes at the airline special services desk or at ticket offices, and there is normally no charge. However, make sure you have any arrangements in writing and your ticket is annotated properly *before* you head to the new departure airport. If you show up without a properly changed ticket, the airline may charge you the one-way fare back home.

● Never pay for anything at the airport, thinking you can write a letter to the customer-service department and get your money back later. Once the airlines have your money, rarely will they return any. If you are told one thing by a telephone agent and another when you arrive at the airport, find a supervisor and sort out any confusion and necessary payments on the spot.

✔ **AIRPORT TIP:** If you have to spend the night at an airport at your own expense, see if the airline can call and get a Distressed Passenger Rate, or ask the hotel manager (decision maker) for it yourself.

DEALING WITH
OVERBOOKING

Most airlines overbook their scheduled flights to a certain extent, and passengers are sometimes left behind or "bumped" as a result. There are two kinds of bumping: voluntary and involuntary.

Voluntary bumping

Almost any group of airline passengers includes some people with urgent travel needs and others who may be more concerned about the cost of their ticket than getting to a destination on time. Department of Transportation (DOT) rules require airlines to seek out people who are willing to give up their seats for some compensation before bumping anyone involuntarily.

Here's how this works: At the check-in or boarding area, airline employees will look for volunteers when it appears that the flight has been oversold. If you're not in a rush to arrive at your next destination, you can trade your time for money or its equivalent (normally a free ticket on a future flight).

But before you do this, you may want to get answers to these important questions:

- When is the next flight on which the airline can confirm your seat? The alternate flight may be just as acceptable to you. On the other hand, if they offer to put you on a wait-list or make you a standby on another flight that's full, you could be stranded.

- Will the airline provide other amenities such as free meals, hotel rooms, telegrams, phone calls, or transportation? If not, you may have to spend the money they offer you on food or lodging while you wait for the next flight.

The DOT has not said how much money the airline has to pay *volunteers*. This means airlines may negotiate with their passengers for an acceptable amount of money—or a free trip or other benefits. Airlines give employees guidelines for bargaining with passengers, and they may select those volunteers willing to sell back their seats for the lowest price.

Denied Boarding Compensation

The most prevalent form of compensation for passengers who are voluntarily bumped is a coupon, sometimes called a Denied Boarding Compensation (DBC) coupon, good for a round-trip flight anywhere within the airline's continental U.S. system (surprisingly, this includes Alaska with some airlines). But check for restrictions.

- These Denied Boarding Compensation coupons are normally good throughout the year, but during high-season blackout periods some airlines may restrict their use by requiring you to wait until the last day before issuing the ticket.

- Some DBC coupons are only for stand-by transportation.

- Some DBC coupons will result in First Class transportation. And many times the airlines will fly passengers who volunteered to be bumped First Class on the next flight, depending on availability.

- **Beware:** When you volunteer to be bumped and are held back from the flight, the flight crew may find a space once a physical passenger count is completed. In this case you will have to get back on your scheduled flight, but without your original seat. This rarely happens, but it has been reported.

Even with free tickets, many times you will hear the airline personnel upping the ante. If originally the airline needed ten volunteers and only five passengers volunteered to be bumped, the gate personnel may offer cash as well. It is like an auction, and they seem to start at $200 plus the free ticket. The top price I have seen while a passenger was $500 and a free ticket, which resulted in almost half the plane volunteering. The first one to the airline representative got the deal. Naturally, everyone who had settled for no cash and only a free ticket, or less than $500, felt mistreated. As my brother says, "That's life on the Ponderosa."

Some fliers have made volunteering to be bumped a part of their check-in routine. As soon as they get to the gate, they ask if the flight is overbooked. If the answer is yes, they let the gate personnel know they are willing to volunteer. This places their name near the top of the list for bumping and a free ticket anywhere on the airline's continental U.S. system. One Sunday after Thanksgiving, I managed three free tickets by successfully volunteering to be bumped from three flights in a row. If you have time, it means free transportation for you and makes life more pleasant for the airline personnel.

Involuntary bumping (U.S.)

Sometimes it doesn't even work to dangle escalating compensation for voluntary bumpees before a packed plane. If there aren't enough volunteers, some folk will be left behind *involuntarily*. This is where the law comes into play.

The DOT requires each airline to give all passengers who are bumped involuntarily a written statement describing their rights and explaining how the carrier decides who gets on an oversold flight and who doesn't. Those travelers who don't get to fly are frequently entitled to an on-the-spot payment. The amount depends on the price of their ticket and the length of the delay.

If you are bumped involuntarily and the airline arranges substitute transportation that is scheduled to get you to your destination (including later connections) within one hour of your original scheduled arrival time, there is no compensation. If the airline arranges substitute transportation that is scheduled to arrive at your destination more than one hour but less than two hours (four hours on international flights) after your original arrival time, the airline must pay you an amount equal to the one-way fare to your final destination, with a $200 maximum. If the substitute transportation is scheduled to get you to your destination more than two hours later (four hours internationally), or if the airline does not make any substitute travel arrangements for you, the compensation doubles (200 percent of the one-way fare, $400 maximum). You always get to keep your original ticket, and you can use it on another flight or have it refunded. The denied boarding compensation is a payment for your inconvenience.

Like all rules, however, there are a few conditions and exceptions:

● To qualify for compensation, you must have a confirmed reservation, and you must have met the airline's deadline for buying your ticket.

● Each airline has a check-in deadline, which is the amount of time before scheduled departure that you must present yourself to the airline at the airport. The deadlines vary; it could be as little as 10 minutes, or longer than 90 minutes. Some airlines merely require you to be at the ticket/baggage counter by this time; others require that you get all the way to the boarding area. There is a separate ticketing deadline (usually at least 30 minutes before departure) for passengers picking up their tickets at the airport. If you miss the ticketing or check-in deadline, you may lose your reservation and your right to compensation if the flight is oversold.

TRAVEL RIGHTS

- As noted above, no compensation is due if the airline arranges substitute transportation scheduled to arrive at your destination within one hour of your original arrival time.

- If the airline substitutes a smaller plane for the one it originally planned to use, the airline isn't required to pay people who are bumped as a result.

- The rules do not apply to charter flights, or to scheduled flights operated with planes that hold 60 or fewer passengers. They don't apply to international flights inbound to the United States, although some airlines on these routes follow them voluntarily. Also, if you are flying between two foreign cities—from Paris to Rome, for example—these rules will not apply (see next section on EC rules).

There are some steps you can take to minimize your chances of being bumped. When you book your reservations or buy your tickets, the agent can tell you what the airline's priorities are for honoring higher priced tickets before boarding people flying on discount fares. Most, however, bump the last people to arrive at the boarding gate. The most effective way to reduce the risk of being bumped is to get to the airport early.

Airlines may offer free transportation on future flights in place of a check for denied boarding compensation. However, you have the right to insist on a check if that is your preference. Once you cash the check (or accept the free flight), you will probably lose the right to demand more money from the airline later on. However, if being bumped costs you more money than the airline will pay you at the airport, you can try to negotiate a higher settlement with their complaint department. If this doesn't work, you usually have 30 days from the date on the check to decide if you want to accept the amount of the check. You are always free to decline the check and take the airline to court to try to obtain more compensation. A recent Supreme Court ruling holds that federal airline regulations do not prevent bumped passengers from suing in state court to recover their financial losses. The DOT's denied boarding regulation only spells out the airlines' *minimum* obligation to people they bump involuntarily.

✔ NOTE: If you get bumped from a flight anywhere other than in the U.S. and Europe, these rules do not necessarily apply. Airlines in some parts of the world offer more special treatment while others offer you none.

Involuntary bumping (European Union)

If your flight originates in the European Union and you find yourself being bumped because of overbooking, you qualify for immediate cash compensation no matter how quickly the airline can get you to your destination. The basic rules are based on the distance of your flight and the length of time you will be delayed. (Compensation listed in ECUs—European Currency Units—equal to US$1.13 at press time):

● For flights *less than 3,500 kilometers* (2,170 miles) with a resulting delay of two hours or less from your scheduled flight you should receive 75ECUs (about $85); if the delay is more than two hours you're due 150ECUs ($170).

● For flights *longer than 3,500 kilometers,* and you will arrive within four hours of your originally scheduled flight, you should receive 150ECUs (about $170); if your delay is more than four hours you get 300ECUs (about $340)

● Your costs for a phone call or fax, normal meals and refreshments that you consume while waiting, and any overnight accommodations necessary must also be paid by the airline.

● The airline may pay you with a voucher for future services, but if you prefer you will be paid with cash.

● Compensation will at no time be more than the price of your ticket.

● If you are traveling on a free ticket or with a charter, you are not entitled to any compensation.

BAGGAGE HANDLING AND PROBLEMS

Between the time you check your luggage and the time you claim it at your destination, it may have passed through a maze of conveyor belts, baggage carts, and forklifts; when airborne, it may have tumbled around the cargo compartment in rough air. In all fairness to the airlines, however, relatively few bags are damaged or lost. With some common-sense packing and other precautions, your bags will probably be among the ones that arrive safely.

You can pack to avoid problems. Some items should never be put into the bag you check into the cargo system—money, jewelry, cameras, medicine, liquids, glass, negotiable securities, or any other things that are valuable, irreplaceable, delicate, or of sentimental value. These and anything else you absolutely need for your trip should be packed in a carry-on bag that will fit under the seat. Remember, the only way to be *sure* your valuables are not damaged or lost is to keep them with you.

Some seasoned travelers recommend carrying enough clothing and personal items with you in carry-on luggage to last 48 hours.

TRAVEL RIGHTS

Baggage limits and excess luggage charges

On domestic flights you are normally limited to two pieces of carry-on luggage and a total of three checked pieces. Again, this varies by airline.

The bags you check should be labeled—inside and out—with your name, address and phone number. Add the name and address of a person to contact at your destination if it's practical. Almost all bags misplaced by airlines do turn up sooner or later. With proper labeling, the bag and its owner can usually be reunited within a few hours.

Some airlines provide boxes for bulky items and garment bags. These boxes help bags arrive intact and are often free for the asking, but may also be available for a nominal fee.

Lock your bags to help prevent pilferage. Remove any shoulder straps and stow them inside, to prevent your bags from getting hung up in the baggage-handing machinery. But if your bags do arrive with broken locks or torn sides, check inside immediately. If something is missing, report it to the airline right away.

If you plan to check any electrical equipment, small appliances, typewriters, pottery, glassware, musical instruments or other fragile items, they should be packed in a container specifically designed to survive rough handling—preferably a factory-sealed carton or a padded hard-shell carrying case.

At check-in, the airline will put baggage destination tags on your luggage and give you the stubs to use as claim checks. Each tag has a three-letter code and flight number that show the baggage sorters on which plane and to which airport your luggage is supposed to go. Double-check the tag and flight number before your bags go down the conveyor belt. (The airline will be glad to tell you the code for your destination when you make reservations or buy your tickets, or at the check-in counter.) Be sure all the tags from previous trips are removed from your bag, since they may confuse busy baggage handlers. Don't lose your claim checks—they are your only proof that you really did check bags with the airline.

Know *where* your bags are checked to. Never assume that your bag will automatically show up at your destination. It may only be heading to an intermediate location!

- Some airlines you may be connecting on do not interline bags (transfer them between airlines).

- Some international flights require baggage to clear customs before your final destination. Local rules may require that you carry your own bag after customs to the transit counter for further connections.

Excess baggage charges can be a big surprise

Airlines use different methods for determining what is and is not excess, and then different calculations to come up with excess baggage charges.

American Airlines provided its excess baggage information:

The limits are three pieces of baggage, whether checked or carried on the aircraft, with a maximum of two carry-ons (with two different specific maximum sizes). Its rules state that a briefcase, garment bag or collapsible luggage cart is considered part of the two-piece allotment. A carry-on pet, while not free, will count as the 45-inch carry-on.

Excess baggage charges are by bag rather than by weight. You can fill up each bag to a 70-pound maximum. The first three bags will cost $45 each; the next three, $65 each; and the seventh and additional bags will cost $130 each. The rules are thereafter based on whether the bags are oversized or weigh more than 70 pounds but less than 100 pounds, and so on . . .

Once the check-in agents decide that you have excess baggage, you can count on forking over a hefty supplement.

On flights in and from the U.S., airlines base excess baggage on a piece system, with a maximum of 70 pounds per piece. Between most other points, excess charges are based on weight.

✔ NOTE: When you are consider what to take with you on a trip, note these things that are considered Free Personal Items:

Purse, overcoat, umbrella, reading material, infant necessities, canes, 35mm type camera (not including camera bag), binoculars, crutches, braces, collapsible walkers, unopened liquor less than 140 proof to be served by flight attendant, one golf club (that fits in overhead compartment), one infant seat or child restraint seat, a collapsible wheelchair or stroller or walker if non-collapsible, or 3-wheel models. Some airlines include a box of fish from Alaska and oranges from Florida in their free allowance.

☛ Musical instruments, not exceeding 39 inches in length, may be transported in place of one of the bags included in free baggage allowance. If the instrument takes you over the three-bag limit or is longer than 39 inches, you must pay excess baggage charges. Large items such as a cello or bass fiddle may require purchase of an additional seat.

☛ Certain sports equipment may also be substituted for one of the free bags. The following equipment qualifies:

Archery equipment, boogie board or knee board, bowling equipment, fishing equipment, golf equipment, hockey or lacrosse sticks, shooting equipment, skateboard, ski equipment, or snowboard. This equipment may exceed 62 inches in length with no oversize charges.

The following sports equipment always is subject to excess baggage charges:

Antlers, empty scuba tank, surfboard, windsurfing equipment, hang-gliding equipment.

Bicycles may be packed in a bag or box. American Airlines sells both bicycle boxes

and bags. The bicycles are then sent for an additional $45 excess luggage charge.

✔ **NOTE:** The above restrictions are from American Airlines. Each airline has its own policy, for example: United Airlines will accept up to 26" bicycles packed by the owner in a bicycle box, which may be purchased from United, as free baggage provided the passengers are within the three-piece limit.

Sending luggage ahead

One trick employed by seasoned travelers is to send their bulky items ahead by UPS, US Post, Federal Express or other shipper. This allows you to avoid the hassles of lugging luggage. Just let the hotel, condominium office, or someone else at your destination know the package is being delivered and ask them to hold it until you arrive. On your return trip you can often call UPS or FedEx and they will pick up your box for its journey home.

✔ The shipping ahead method comes in especially handy when dealing with bulky children's items for a winter trip.

Carry-on baggage notes

According to the DOT there is no single federal standard for carry-on baggage, so check with the airline for any limits it places on the *size, weight* and *number* of carry-on bags.

- Inquire about your specific flights. The limitations vary depending on the type of aircraft.

- Check for each airline you are flying. Rules vary from one to another.

- Garment bag space is not unlimited, so some may have to be checked. Garment bags left in the front closet are not considered checked baggage.

- During holidays, especially the Sunday after Thanksgiving and the Sunday after Christmas, under-seat and above-seat capacity are pushed to their limits. Plan to carry less onto the plane with you and board early.

Baggage liability limits excess insurance

If your bags are delayed, lost or damaged on a domestic flight, the airline may invoke a $1,250 *per passenger* ceiling on the amount of money they'll pay you. When your luggage and its contents are worth more than that, you may want to purchase Excess Valuation, if available, from the airline as you check in. This will increase the carrier's potential liability.

> Excess Valuation Insurance is sold by the airlines for $1 to $2 for each $100 of coverage. There is normally a limit of $5000 on this excess coverage. Check carefully to see exactly what the airlines do and do not cover, especially if you are traveling with a computer, art, antiques or other valuables.

The airline may refuse to sell excess valuation on some items that are especially valuable or breakable, such as antiques, musical instruments, jewelry, manuscripts, negotiable securities and cash. Whatever is not covered by the airline's insurance normally can be covered by your household goods insurance or a personal effects policy.

These policies vary greatly and rarely cover items such as computers or anything associated with your business. Business owners should carefully review their insurance policies to make sure that portable computers are insured against loss and damage. Also, anyone traveling with portable computers should keep backup disks separate from the computer.

Your claim must be supported by receipts. The airlines will only reimburse you for the depreciated value of items lost. You will not get replacement value.

✔ NOTE: Some insurance professionals suggest that you submit an insurance claim against your household insurance first rather than making your claim against the airline. Your household insurance company will then deal with the airline. This helps in two ways—many policies cover replacement values (the airlines never do) and your insurance company probably has more clout with the airlines than you do.

> CREDIT CARD HOLDERS NOTE: Both American Express and Diners Club charge cards provide excess baggage insurance offering extra protection. See page 123 for more information or call your cardmember service number.

The Warsaw Convention treaty and rules

On international trips, liability limits are set by the Warsaw Convention, a 1920s treaty regulating air commerce. Unless you buy excess valuation, the liability limits are 250 French gold francs per kilo (a kilo is about 2.2 pounds) of checked baggage, and the airlines have a formula for converting this limit into U.S. dollars. For example, as of press time, the limit was $9.07 per pound or $20 per kilo or about $640 *per bag* on international flights.

The Warsaw Convention also says that the airline must note your baggage weight on your airline ticket for you to take advantage of the liability limit. This way, if you file a claim, there will be a record of the weight on which to base the settlement. Some airlines write the total weight on the ticket at check-in time. Others explain in their notices that, if they lose or damage your luggage, they will assume that each checked bag weighs 32 kilos (70 pounds) for purposes of calculating that carrier's liability. In either case, it's a good idea to read the baggage notice on your ticket before you check your bags.

Damaged bags

If your suitcase arrives smashed or torn, the airline will usually pay for repairs. If it can't be fixed, they will negotiate a settlement to pay you its depreciated value. The same holds true for clothing and items packed inside. Report external damage before you leave the airport. Insist on filling out a form.

Get the phone number for the *local* airline baggage services office. They are your best contact if you plan on having the bag repaired or replaced immediately.

Airlines may decline to pay for damage caused by the fragile nature of the broken item or your carelessness in packing. Airlines may also refuse to give you money for your damaged items inside the bag when there's no evidence of external damage to the suitcase, especially if it is soft-sided luggage. But airlines should not disclaim liability for fragile merchandise in the original factory sealed carton, a cardboard mailing tube, or other container designed for shipping and packed with protective padding material, or for goods packed in hard-sided luggage.

When you check in, airline personnel should let you know if they think your suitcase or package may not survive the trip intact. Before accepting a questionable item, they will ask you to sign a statement in which you agree to check it at your own risk. But even if you do sign this form, the airline should pay for damage caused by its own negligence, shown by external injury to the suitcase or package.

Delayed bags

If you and your suitcase don't connect at your destination, don't panic. The airlines have very sophisticated systems that track down about 98 percent of the bags they misplace and return them to their owners within hours.

If your bags don't come off the conveyor belt, report this to the airline *before* you leave the airport. You must fill out a form describing the bag, listing its contents (be as accurate as possible: this is the listing that any payments will be based upon), and providing other identification information for the baggage-tracing staff. Be sure to keep a copy of this form for your records.

To cover your a-double-q have the airline fill out a form even if they say the bag will be on the next flight. Make sure to get the appropriate phone number for baggage service, not the reservations number. And get the name of the person who took the report.

Airlines will go to great lengths to deliver any delayed bags to you in your destination city at your home, hotel or other accommodation. The delay is usually only a few hours.

If the delay is longer, the airlines will generally absorb reasonable expenses you incur while they look for your missing belongings. You and the airline may have different ideas of what's reasonable, however, and the amount they will pay is subject to negotiation. Normally, the airlines consider basic clothing and toiletries as reasonable.

Most carriers set guidelines for their airport employees that allow them to disburse some money at the airport for emergency purchases. The amount depends on whether or not you're away from home and how long it takes to track down and return your bags.

If the airline does not give you a cash advance, be reasonable in what you buy if your bags are delayed. Purchase only necessities and keep all receipts.

If the airline misplaces sporting equipment such as skis or scuba equipment for use on a vacation, it will sometimes pay for the rental of replacements. For replacement clothing, the carrier may offer to absorb only a portion of the purchase cost, arguing that you will be able to use the new clothes in the future. However, they will often pay for rental clothing if you can locate a shop making such rentals.

When you've checked in fresh foods or any other perishable goods and they are ruined because their delivery is delayed, the airline won't reimburse you. Airlines may be liable if they lose or damage perishable items, but they won't accept responsibility for spoilage caused by temporary loss.

Airlines are liable for provable consequential damages (up to the $1,250 limit on domestic flights and $9.07 per pound limit on international flights, and whatever excess valuation you purchased) in connection with the delay. If you can't resolve the claim with the airline's airport staff, keep a record of the names of the employees with whom you dealt, and hold on to all travel documents and receipts for any money you spent in connection with the mishandling. (It's okay to surrender your baggage claim tags to the airline when you fill out a form at the airport, as long as you get a copy of the form and it notes that you gave up the tags.) Call or write the airline's consumer office when you get home. If you still do not get satisfaction from the airline, contact DOT (see page 137).

Late luggage

If you arrive late for a flight, airlines often will want you to sign a Late Baggage Tag. Signing this ticket means that you accept all responsibility for the luggage not arriving at the same time you arrive. You will also be expected to pick up your luggage at the destination airport.

If you are running late for a flight your best bet is to carry your luggage with you to the gate and hand it to baggage handlers there. Many airlines will tag your bags at check-in so that you can just hand them to the gate personnel.

Lost luggage

Once your bag is declared officially lost, you will have to submit a claim. Some airlines will proceed using the form that you filled out when your bag was only thought to be delayed; others may require you to fill out a different form.

✔ **Check on this:** failure to complete the second form when required could delay your claim. The airline will usually refer your claim form to a central office, and the negotiations between you and the airline will begin.

Airlines don't automatically pay the full amount of every claim they receive. They use the information on your form to estimate the value of your lost belongings, and like insurance companies, they consider the depreciated value of your possessions, not their replacement costs.

If you're tempted to exaggerate your claim, don't. Airlines may completely deny claims they feel are inflated or fraudulent. They often ask for sales receipts and other documentation to back up claims, especially if a large amount of money is involved. If you don't keep extensive records, you can expect to dicker with the airline over the value of your goods.

Generally, it takes an airline anywhere from six weeks to three months to pay you for your lost luggage. During this waiting period, you should stay in touch with the company both to show your concern and to be sure they're following up on your claim. Even though the airlines lose relatively few bags, when they lose yours, you'll want to keep a watchful eye on the treatment of your claim.

SMOKING RULES

Domestic flights

Under U.S. government rules, cigar and pipe smoking are banned on commercial aircraft. In addition, all smoking is prohibited on all domestic flights (including Puerto Rico and the Virgin Islands), except for flights to or from Alaska or Hawaii with a scheduled flight time of six hours or more.

International flights

The following rules apply to cigarette smoking on U.S. airlines flying internationally—both scheduled and charter.

● The airline must provide a seat in a non-smoking section to every passenger who asks for one, as long as the passenger complies with the carrier's seat assignment deadline and procedures. (Therefore, standby passengers do not have this right.)

● If necessary, the airline must expand the non-smoking section to accommodate the passengers described above.

● The airline doesn't have provide you a non-smoking seat with your traveling companion, and you don't have the right to specify a window or aisle non-smoking seat.

● Smoke drifting from the smoking section into the non-smoking section is not a violation.

● No smoking is allowed while an aircraft is on the ground or when the ventilation system is not fully functioning.

● **Never smoke in airplane restrooms.**
Smoking was banned in all but the designated smoking sections after 116 people were killed in only four minutes, apparently because a smoker left a burning cigarette butt in the trash bin.

● **Don't smoke while standing.**
In the event of air turbulence your lighted cigarette may end up burning someone (expect a liability suit) or starting a fire.

▲ FYI: Foreign airlines flying internationally don't have to follow these rules, but most of them offer non-smoking sections anyway. About three dozen countries now ban smoking on all or some domestic flights. Almost a third of these countries are in Europe, and the United Nations has just passed an agreement (not legally binding) which will ban smoking on all international flights starting in July 1996, signifying the potential end of inflight smoking. If avoiding smoke is important to you, ask the airlines about their smoking policies.

On-board health
CONSIDERATIONS

✈ **Dehydration:** Aircraft cabin air is
   about the driest we experience. To com-
   bat dehydration, which often causes
   headaches, coughing, itchy skin and
   sore eyes, you should drink a glass of
   water every hour. Also try to avoid
   drinking alcoholic beverages and salty
   snacks, since they increase
   dehydration. (Coffee, tea, and such
   caffeinated soft drinks as Coke and
   Pepsi also promote dehydration.)
   Don't wear contact lenses—they are
   normally very uncomfortable in super-
   dry air. If you must wear contacts, bring
   plenty of rewetting solution.

✈ **Recycled air:** This has caused much dis-
   cussion, but recent studies show that the
   airlines' policy of limited recycling of
   air has no measurable effect on passengers' health.

✈ **Traveling with a cold:** This is not a
   good idea, but sometimes inevitable.
   Take a decongestant about an hour
   before takeoff and again 45 minutes
   before landing to help ease ear
   blockage and sinus agony.

CHARTER RIGHTS

Charter flights are governed by rules far different from those that regulate scheduled airline carriers. For every dollar you save, there may be another price to pay. Often charter prices are only a few dollars less than those of scheduled airlines. This next section was published by the DOT as part of its Plane Talk series to tell consumers what "Charter" really entails. It does not take a rocket scientist to see that these rules favor the charter operators and not the passengers.

Over the past few years, charter flights have been relaxed to make lower cost air transportation available to more people. Public Charters can be purchased from a tour operator, a travel agent, or sometimes directly from the airline.

If your flight has been arranged by a club or other organization for its members it may be what is called an affinity charter flight. These charters generally do not carry the consumer protection provisions of Public Charters. Be sure you know what kind of charter flight you are purchasing.

A Public Charter may include only the flight, or it may be sold as a complete package, including hotels, guided tours, and ground transportation. Either way, your rights are spelled out in a contract you have with the tour operator. The operator or your travel agent should give you a contract to sign at the time you purchase your trip. read it before you pay any money.

The Department of Transportation requires tour operators to disclose certain information in your contract about the restrictions that they impose and also rights that you have under DOT rules:

☐ **You usually pay penalties if you cancel.** The closer to departure you cancel, the bigger the penalty. On some charters, if a substitute can go in your place you only lose a $25 fee.

☐ **You can buy trip cancellation insurance.** These policies usually provide a refund in case you must cancel owing to illness or death in the family. Your travel agent or tour operator can tell you how to buy the insurance and what health conditions it does or doesn't cover. Charter cancellation insurance often won't pay you if you must cancel because of a preexisting condition.

☐ **The tour operator or airline can cancel a Public Charter for any reason up until 10 days before departure.** Your flight might be canceled if it doesn't sell well or for some other reason. This is a risk you take in return for a low fare. (During the last 10 days before departure, a Public Charter can be canceled only if it is physically impossible to operate it.)

❑ **All charter flights and ground arrangements are subject to changes.** Signing a contract does not guarantee that prices won't go up or that itineraries won't change. But, if there is a *major change* in your flight or tour, *you have the right to cancel and get a penalty-free refund.*

Major changes include:
- A change in departure or return city (not including a simple change in the order in which cities are visited).
- A change in departure or return date, unless the date change results from a flight delay. (However, a flight delay more than 48 hours is a major change.)
- A substitution of a hotel that was not named as an alternative hotel in your contract.
- An increase in price, if the total of all increases billed to you is more than 10 percent of what you originally paid. (No increases are allowed during the last 10 days before departure.)

If your tour operator notifies you of a major change before departure, you get a full refund if you decide to cancel. If you choose not to cancel, the operator is not required to make partial refunds. However, if you don't find out about a change until after your trip has begun, you can reject the changed flight or hotel, make and pay for your own alternative plans, and insist on a refund for the changed component when you get home.

❑ **No "open returns" are allowed on round-trip public charters.** Be sure you have a specific return date, city and flight, so you won't be stranded.

❑ **The tour operator has to take specific steps to protect your money.** The tour operator must have a surety agreement, such as a bond, and must usually have an escrow account at a bank that holds your money until your flight takes place. If your money is going into a charter escrow account, the bank will be named in your contract, and the check that is sent to the charter operator should be made payable to that bank. (If you are using a travel agent, it's OK for you to make your check out to that agent; he will make his check payable to the escrow account.) Identify the departure date and destination on the face of the check. If a tour operator goes out of business you should contact the surety company or bank identified in your contract for a refund.

❑ **You alone are responsible for knowing if you need a visa and passport for your trip.** You can be certain of the visa and passport rules of the countries you plan to visit by calling or writing their embassies in

Washington, D.C., or their consulates in some major U.S. cities.

❏ **If your luggage gets lost during your tour, there may be a dispute over who is liable.** The charter airlines process claims for bags that were lost or damaged while in their possession. If it is not clear where the problem occurred (e.g. between the airport and a hotel), the operator and the airline may both decline liability. To cover yourself, find out if your renter's or homeowner's insurance policy covers losses that happen when you're away from home. You might also ask your travel agent if there's a one-shot baggage insurance policy available to cover baggage problems while you are on your charter trip.

❏ **Your charter may be delayed.** Last minute schedule changes and departure delays of several hours are not uncommon on charters. A flight can be delayed up to 48 hours before the charter operator must offer you the option to cancel with a full refund.

❏ **Charters and scheduled flights operate independently of each other.** If there's a delay on the scheduled flight connecting you to the city where your charter departs, causing you to miss your charter, you lose your flight and money. Charter reservations are only good for one flight. If you miss it for any reason, you're probably out of luck. Check with the tour operator to

**TRAVEL
RIGHTS**

see if he has another charter flying to your destination.

If your charter is late returning and causes you to miss a scheduled connecting flight back to your home, you have to pay your own expense while you wait for the next connection. If you have a discount fare on a scheduled connecting flight you could lose it if the returning charter is delayed. Then you, not the airline or tour operator, have to pay more for a regular non-discount fare.

Your baggage can't be checked through from a scheduled flight to a charter, and vice-versa. You have to claim your baggage and re-check it yourself. When planning a charter, allow plenty of time to check in at the airport from which your charter leaves, or from which you have a connecting flight. On international trips, remember that you may encounter delays in Customs.

❑ **You might find the seating on your charter plane more crowded than you're used to.** The low charter rate depends in part on spreading costs over a large number of people with virtually all of the seats being filled.

❑ **If a charter flight hasn't sold out shortly before departure, the operator can sell seats at bargain basement prices to latecomers.** Some who have paid the regular price well in advance may object, but should realize that the operator's alternative may be to cancel the flight altogether for economic reasons.

❑ **Charter rates are relatively low, but may not be the cheapest fare to your destination.** Ask your travel agent to compare fares on scheduled and charter flights for you.

Charters offer nonstop flights for an affordable price. They can be a wise travel investment if you can be flexible in your travel plans. Just be sure you know the conditions for the trip you're buying before you pay for it. Questions? Call DOT at 202-366-2220.

✔ **AUTHOR'S NOTE:** My vote is to pay the small amount of extra money needed to take a scheduled flight.

✈ ✈ ✈ **AIRLINE FACT** ✈ ✈ ✈
The world's largest airport terminal is Hartsfield Atlanta International Airport, Georgia, with floor space covering over 50 acres. It has a capacity for handling 75 million passengers a year.
✈ ✈ ✈ ✈ ✈ ✈ ✈ ✈ ✈ ✈ ✈

PET RIGHTS*

Over two million pets and other live animals are transported by air every year in the United States. Federal and state governments impose restrictions on transporting live animals. In addition, each airline establishes its own company policy for the proper handling of the animals they transport. As a shipper or owner you also have a responsibility to take the necessary precautions to ensure the well-being of the animal you ship.

Because each airline establishes its own policy, it is important to check with the air carrier you intend to use. However, the following are some of the provisions you will probably encounter at most airlines.

> Airlines generally require health certificates from all shippers. So it's a good idea to have a licensed veterinarian examine animals within ten days prior to shipment and issue a certificate stating that the animal is in good health.

*From Plane Talk, written by the U.S. Department of Transportation

The **Animal and Plant Health Inspection Service of the U.S. Department of Agriculture** enforces the Federal Animal Welfare Act. Here are several of the more important requirements.

- Dogs and cats must be at least eight weeks old and must have been weaned for at least five days.

- Cages and other containers must meet the minimum standard for size, ventilation, strength, sanitation and design for safe handling. (Sky kennels furnished by the airlines meet these requirements.)

- Dogs and cats must not be brought to the airline for shipping more than four hours before departure. (Six hours is permitted if shipping arrangements are made in advance.)

- If puppies or kittens less than 16 weeks of age are in transit more than 12 hours, food and water must be provided. Older animals must have food at least every 24 hours and water at least every 12 hours. Written instructions for food and water must accompany all animals shipped, regardless of the scheduled time in transit.

- Animals may not be exposed to temperatures less than 45 degrees Fahrenheit unless they are accompanied by a certificate signed by a veterinarian stating that they are acclimated to lower temperatures.

- Animals cannot be shipped COD unless the shipper guarantees the return freight should the animals be refused at destination.

Transporting pets as baggage

A pet may be transported as baggage if accompanied on the same flight to the same destination. Some air carriers may impose a special fee or excess baggage charge for this service. Pets may be shipped as cargo if unaccompanied, and many airline cargo departments employ specialists in the movement of animals. Animals must always be shipped in pressurized holds. Some airlines allow the kennel to be carried in the passenger cabin as carry-on luggage if it fits under the seat.

→ In addition to compliance with federal regulations and airline company policy, there are a number of precautions the owner/shipper can take to ensure the welfare of a shipped pet.

- Before traveling, accustom your pet to the kennel in which it will be shipped.

- Do not give your pet solid food in the six hours prior to the flight, although a moderate amount of water and a walk before and after the flight are advised.

- Be sure to reserve a space for your pet in advance, and inquire about time and location for drop-off and pick-up.

- Try to schedule a nonstop flight; avoid connections and the heavy travel of a holiday or weekend flight.

- Inquire about any special health requirements such as quarantine for overseas travel (including Hawaii).

- Be sure to put your name and the recipient's name, address and phone number in large letters on the kennel.

✔ With careful planning, your pet will arrive safely at its destination.

✈ ✈ ✈ **AIRLINE FACT** ✈ ✈ ✈
The first airline to transport animals was KLM Royal Dutch Airlines—in 1924 a prize bull named Nico made history. The flight was between Rotterdam and Paris.
✈ ✈ ✈ ✈ ✈ ✈ ✈ ✈ ✈ ✈ ✈ ✈

TRAVEL
RIGHTS

Pet shipping problems

You may want to think twice about shipping your pet as baggage. Recent reports indicate that for all the regulation, the pets are having a rather hard time, in very hot weather.

News stories have revealed shocking cases of pet handling problems—56 puppies died on a TWA flight; 32 dogs died on a Delta flight; 24 dogs passed away on a United Airlines flight; and five dogs died on American Airlines. The Humane Society of America has received complaints about every major airline in the country.

Court cases have held that a pet that dies during a flight, even if by extreme cold or extreme heat under the airline's control, is, *leagally speaking*, nothing more than a piece of checked baggage. Pets are subject to the same lost/damaged baggage rules that dictate the monetary damages to be paid on your old suitcase (see pages 61-69). As the American Airlines spokesman so delicately puts it, "an animal is checked baggage from a legal liability standpoint."

Pet rights vs. passenger rights

Most of these regulations serve to allow transportation of pets. What happens when a passenger is allergic to a pet that has been brought aboard as hand baggage? This happened to a passenger recently traveling on a full flight. She learned that the pet's right to fly was more important than her right to breathe comfortably. Her only alternatives were to exchange her seat with a non-allergic passenger or to deplane (without compensation) and catch a later flight.

If the pet has been properly booked on the flight as carry-on baggage, it can fly and is treated with the same rights as its owner.

The moral of the story: If you have an allergic reaction to animals, let the reservationist know, or if you see a pet being carried aboard speak immediately with the gate personnel so they can maneuver to find you a seat out of harm's way.

✈ ✈ ✈ **AIRLINE FACT** ✈ ✈ ✈

The world's busiest airport is Chicago International Airport, O'Hare Field with a takeoff or landing every 40.4 seconds around the clock.

✈ ✈ ✈ ✈ ✈ ✈ ✈ ✈ ✈ ✈ ✈

Auto rights

I n the past few years, the world of automobile rentals has become much more complicated.

What many took for granted—multiple drivers, inclusive liability insurance, and the ability to rent a car as long as you had a valid driver's license—has changed and is not always part of the rental agreement.

What many knew was not ever included in rental agreements, such as collision damage insurance, now is included—to a greater or lesser extent—if certain credit cards are used to rent certain types of cars in certain circumstances for a certain length of time if driven along certain types of roads.

None of this is complex until you end up in an accident or have to modify a reservation at the last minute. Or until you are faced with a rental agent who looks you straight in the eye and tells you your credit card collision damage waiver (CDW) insurance doesn't cover the automobile you are planning to rent. (At least he or she "can't guarantee that the car is covered" or they "wouldn't want to chance it.")

Naturally, none of us wants to "chance it" with massive liabilities. So read on.

Collision damage insurance

In this section we deal with the most common source of confusion for automobile renters—collision damage waiver (CDW) or loss-damage waiver (LDW). There are several basics:

❑ Most people who rent automobiles do not need to pay for the additional collision damage insurance. They have other coverage which in effect duplicates the expensive rental car company insurance.

❑ If you have your own automobile insurance with collision coverage, you probably have enough liability insurance to meet most legal challenges and most small collisions. However, most personal automobile policies limit the amount of damages paid to the value of your *personal* car. Check with your insurance company to find out exactly what their coverage is on rental cars.

❑ Most Visa Gold and Gold MasterCard credit cards, some normal credit cards, Diners Club and American Express provide a form of CDW.

❑ Credit cards provide one of two types of coverage—

Primary coverage means that while you are renting a car according to the card rules, the credit card insurance is your primary insurance. If you have an accident, your own insurance will not be responsible for any payments.

Secondary coverage (the most prevalent form) means that in case of an accident your own automobile insurance company is responsible for initial insurance payments and the credit card will pay any excess not covered by your personal auto insurance.

How credit card CDW works

The collision damage waiver you get with your credit card is not the same as purchasing CDW from the rental company.

The rental company CDW releases you from any liability in case of accident. With credit card CDW you are personally responsible for any damages: in some cases you must pay the car-rental company for the damages and will be reimbursed by your credit card company. In other situations the credit card company will pay the damages directly to the car-rental company—they are paying your bill.

If, in case of an accident, you cannot afford to make a short-term damage payment until you are reimbursed by your personal automobile insurance and the credit card company, you may be better off paying for the CDW sold by the rental-car company.

Once you know what your insurance covers and you decide to use your credit card collision insurance, you activate the insurance by charging the rental against your credit card and declining all insurance offered by the rental car company.

NOTE: Credit card company policies vary significantly, not only in their primary and secondary coverage, but also in length of rental that is insured. The basic rule seems to be that automobile rentals here in the U.S. are covered up to 15 days. Foreign rentals are covered for 15 to 30 days, so make sure your collision damage insurance will last as long as your planned rental.

☛ If you use a **Diners Club** card you are covered worldwide with full value **primary insurance for 29 days.**

☛ MasterCard BusinessCard provides full-value **primary collision/loss damage insurance,** but only for 15 days.

Credit card CDW programs

❑ As noted above, most credit cards provide secondary insurance coverage. Several charge cards offer primary coverage, but their numbers are dwindling. Check the fine print in your card agreement to find out what type of coverage your card provides.

❑ Diners Club and MasterCard BusinessCard are the only cards that offers full-value primary insurance to all card holders. Recently Visa has also announced a business card with primary insurance.

❑ Check carefully to find out whether the CDW provided by your credit card will cover additional drivers listed on the rental contract. Also see whether the credit cards provide loss of revenue coverage, which reimburses the rental car company for any revenue lost while the car is being repaired.

❑ Check with your credit card issuer to find out which automobile models are covered by their policy.

> **Note: There are many differences in credit-card collision damage coverage.**

Credit card CDW provides a lesson in the importance of reading the fine print. Though credit card companies never talk about the differences in their rental collision policies, they can make a big difference in deciding which card to use.

❏ If you are renting a Mercedes or BMW you'll have to use the AT&T Visa Gold or Diners Club; the other cards don't provide coverage.

❏ If you are planning a trip in a mini-van and don't know which make of vehicle you'll get from the rental company, use Diners Club or AT&T Gold MasterCard—all mini-vans are covered.

❏ If you are going to rent a sport/utility vehicle such as a Jeep Renegade, Jeep Cherokee, Chevrolet Blazer, Ford Bronco or Suzuki Samurai and plan to drive it only on paved roads, use the American Express Card or Diners Club—they give complete coverage.

→ **CitiBank MasterCard BusinessCard does not cover:**

"Rental of trucks, campers, jeep-type vehicles, trailers, off-road vehicles, motorbikes, recreational vehicles, vans or mini-vans mounted on a truck chassis (call the MasterCard Assistance Center before renting a van or mini-van to confirm whether the vehicle is covered), antique cars (which means cars that are over 20 years old or have not been manufactured for 10 or more years), limousines, expensive or exotic cars (for example, Corvette, Mercedes Benz, Porsche, Jaguar; call the MasterCard Assistance Center before renting a car to confirm whether the vehicle is covered); except that restrictions on exotic or expensive cars do not apply to cars rented outside the United States."

✦ AUTOMOBILE FACT ✦

The worst exit to miss on an interstate highway is Exit 41 (Knolls, Utah) on I-80 with 37.7 miles to the next exit, Exit 4 (Bonneville Speedway, Utah).

→ **American Express Corporate Card does not cover the following vehicles:**

- Expensive cars, valued at over $40,000 (restrictions on expensive, exotic or antique cars do not apply to cars rented outside the U.S., its territories and possessions).
- Exotic cars, such as Aston Martin, Bentley, Bricklin, Cadillac Fleetwood Limo, Daimler, DeLorean, Excalibur, Ferrari, Jensen, Lamborghini, Lincoln Limo, Rolls Royce, Porsche, or similar vehicle;
- Antique cars (over 20 years old or not manufactured for 10 or more years);
- Off-road vehicles, motorcycles, mopeds, recreational vehicles, trucks, campers, trailers, certain vans, and any other vehicle which is not a rental car;
- Mini-vans which are used for commercial hire. (Mini-vans are covered when rented for personal and business use only).
- Four-wheel drive sport/utility vehicles when driven off-road. (Four-wheel drive vehicles, including but not limited to Jeep Renegade, Jeep Cherokee, Chevrolet Blazer, Ford Bronco and Suzuki Samurai, are covered when driven on paved roads.)

TRAVEL
RIGHTS

→ **AT&T Universal Cards (both the standard Visa and MasterCard)** do not cover the following vehicles:

"Rental of trucks, trailers, off-road vehicles, sport utility vehicles (for example, Jeep Wrangler, Ford Explorer, or Suzuki Samurai), recreational vehicles, motorbikes, campers, vans or mini-vans mounted on a truck chassis, antique cars (which means cars that are over 20 years old or have not been manufactured for 10 or more years), limousines, or expensive or exotic cars (for example Corvette, Mercedes Benz, Porsche, or Jaguar). Call AT&T Universal Card Service at 800-423-4343 before renting a car, van or mini-van to confirm whether the vehicle is covered. Restrictions on exotic or expensive cars do not apply to cars rented outside the U.S."

→ **AT&T Universal Card Gold MasterCard** covers "all mini-vans," otherwise coverage is virtually identical.

→ **AT&T Visa Gold** provides significant modifications stating:

"Certain mini-vans (such as Dodge Caravan, Plymouth Voyager, and Chevrolet Lumina) manufactured and designed to transport a maximum of six passengers and used exclusively for the transportation of passengers are also covered. Vans other than six-passenger mini-vans are not covered. Rental autos do not include trucks, off-road vehicles, motorcycles, mopeds, motorbikes, recreational vehicles, sport utility vehicles, campers or trailers. Pickup trucks and minibuses are not covered. Off-road vehicles are excluded worldwide. An off-road vehicle is a sport utility vehicle such as a Jeep Renegade, Suzuki Samurai or any other similar vehicles designed and manufactured primarily for off-road use." The expensive, exotic and antique cars are excluded as above with a major difference—BMW, Mercedes Benz, Cadillac and Lincoln are neither considered exotic nor expensive (limousines, four-wheel drives and vans of these particular models are not covered).

Other credit card insurance limitations

❑ Your credit card collision damage insurance does not cover any damage to the *other* car. The American Express Corporate Card Description of Coverage states, "For example in the event of a collision involving the

Cardmember's rental car, damage to the other driver's car or the injury of anyone or anything are not covered."

❏ If you get into an accident and it can be proved that you were intoxicated (with drugs *or* alcohol), many credit card collision damage policies, such as the American Express, Diners Club, and those of AT&T Universal Card, will not pay any claims. The MasterCard BusinessCard policy doesn't mention that factor.

Liability coverage

Although collision damage is limited to the value of a vehicle you might total, liability for personal injury is virtually unlimited and therefore much more significant. Unfortunately, the laws covering personal injury are as varied as the states. Everything—vehicle ownership, driver negligence, mechanical failure, and more—comes into play. There are no absolutes, except that you should make sure you are covered in some way.

Once upon a time full, primary liability insurance was included in all car-rental contracts, but that has changed. Today, in some states, even the largest car rental companies only provide secondary liability coverage. That is, they pick up your coverage when your personal insurance is exhausted.

This pattern is spreading. Take time to find out what liability coverage is provided when you make your reservations and be ready to make sure you have adequate liability coverage.

Liability/collision insurance limitations on personal automobile policies

On the personal automobile insurance side of the question, some insurance companies are now starting to eliminate the automatic inclusion of collision and liability coverage for policy holders who travel on business.

Make sure to check your policy carefully. Coverage varies on a state-by-state basis. This additional rental car coverage for business travel is often available only as an optional rider.

✦ AUTOMOBILE FACT ✦
The world's first license plates were introduced by Paris police in France in 1893.

TRAVEL
RIGHTS

Negotiating rental car rates

Rental car rates are as complicated as airline rates. In addition to daily, weekly, weekend, sub-compact, compact, mid-sized, and so forth, renters have to deal with frequent-flier rates, automobile club rates, and other special promotional rates. If you don't already have a good idea of what rate you want to pay, your chances of getting the lowest rate are significantly diminished.

Most automobile rental agents will not inform potential renters of the lowest rates available unless prompted by references to specific promotional rates quoted from newspapers or frequent-flier brochures.

Large associations like USAA and AAA have negotiated rates which are a bargain if you must rent a car on short notice during the week. However, these negotiated rates are not as big a bargain as many of the promotional and weekend rates car rental ads tout.

✔ With rental car rates, research is as important as with airline tickets, even more so—airline reservationists will almost always offer the lowest rate on a given flight on a specific day. Rental car reservationists must be carefully prompted to surrender the lowest rate.

Some of the best rates available are through airline frequent-flier programs or associated with the airline upon which you arrive at the airport where you will be picking up your car. Reservationists have told me that great deals are available to members of wholesale clubs such as Sam's or COSTCO.

Once you have made a reservation with a rental car company for a specific car at a specific rate, they are committed to providing you that rate, but not necesserily that size car. For example, if after making a reservation for a compact, you arrive and no compacts are available, the rental car company must provide you another car of the same or greater size for the same rate. If only smaller cars are available, the rental car company should make that car available at a reduced rate based on your *original* rental rate.

Again, everything is up for negotiation and depends to a large degree on the manager on duty and your bargaining skills.

Screening driver's licenses

A new twist to automobile rentals is a growing system of screening driving records. Yes, 1984 has definitely arrived at Hertz, Avis and Budget even if it is about a decade late. Now these car rental companies screen the Department of Motor Vehicles (DMV) records of drivers requesting a rental car in a growing number of states including New York, Maryland, Florida, California, Ohio and Washington, D.C. Yes, the rental company computer accesses your home state driving record from the DMV computers.

Everyone gets checked. And as more state DMVs computerize, this practice is sure to spread.

✔ If you have had an accident within the last two years the companies may refuse to rent you a car based on their criteria—basically, if there was any personal injury or a fatality you will be out of luck. Most rental firms are creating a blacklist, so if you are refused rental in one state, you will probably be refused rental everywhere.

If you are with a client on a business trip, this may be downright embarrassing.

✔ NOTE: Driver's licenses are checked when you show up to rent the car rather than at the time of the reservation. This makes getting another car from another

company, especially another car at a
similar rate, difficult, if indeed possible.

- ❑ When you are refused a rental you
  have no tested rights—even if the
  DMV records are in error.

- ❑ Check your driving record at your state
  DMV.

- ❑ Ask before you arrive at the rental
  counter whether the auto rental
  company screens driver's licenses.

- ❑ If you have been found unfit for a rental
  because of a license check you will
  have to find a company which does not
  check licenses. Call your DMV and find
  out what you can do to clear your
  record. But be aware, in some states
  there is no erasing any accident record.

In the rental companies' defense, these
checks were prompted by liability laws in
New York, Florida and about ten other
states which have vicarious liability laws
that hold the automobile owner
responsible for the damages caused by it,
even when operated by someone else.
Unfortunately what began as a defense
against massive personal-injury awards in
a few states has spread to affect all of us.

Additional driver rules and charges

❑ Many rental car companies now charge up to an additional $5 per additional driver *per day*. If you are renting a car and plan to share the driving, make sure to check out additional driver charges. They can come as a surprise at the car rental counter, and can ruin what appeared to be a good deal.

❑ These additional driver charges vary greatly between states. Some Hertz and Avis locations charge nothing for additional drivers; other charge $5 per rental and yet others assess up to $10 per day. Hertz waives additional driver charges for all AAA members. Some locations charge for additional drivers under 25 years of age but don't charge for other additional drivers. Some rental companies charge for spouses and family members, others don't.

NOTE: When you rent a car, every additional driver must be on the rental form or it must be clearly stated that "immediate family members may drive the automobile" or something to that effect. If not, any collision damage or liability insurance is null and void in case of an accident by a driver not recorded on the form.

Check your rental car
Basics to look for

What happens if you have a flat tire and the spare is also flat, or the lug wrench is missing? Or what can the rental car company do for you when you reach the top of a mountain pass and find that the snow chains provided are the wrong size—worse yet, too small? What if you discover, after parking for lunch, a crumpled fender you didn't notice before you left the lot?

In these cases you are normally up the proverbial creek without a paddle. So protect yourself and check out any car you are getting ready to rent.

❑ Check the spare and make sure you have the basic automobile tool kit with the lug wrench and jack.

❑ If you are picking up chains, carefully insure that they are the proper ones for your tires.

❑ Do a walk-around and check for broken lights, scratches and dents, or other damage you may be held responsible for.

❑ Note which side the fuel filler door is on. This is only a little thing, but can ease hassles at your first filling station.

**TRAVEL
RIGHTS**

- ❑ If you are paying for mileage make sure to check the odometer and note the level of the gas tank. If mileage doesn't match the rental form, or if the tank isn't full, let the attendant know.

- ❑ If there is anything else amiss, have it repaired or noted on the rental agreement before you leave the lot.

Rental car breakdowns

What happens if your rental car transmission freezes in reverse, or you lose power and find yourself stranded on the highway, or the engine just won't start?

This is where bigger really is better. The larger rental agencies such as Hertz, Avis, Budget or National can provide a real advantage over the smaller ones. Since the large companies have more rental locations, it is easier to get another car and to get help. Other large agencies like Alamo or Dollar can also provide good assistance, depending on how close you are to one of their offices. Smaller agencies with fewer locations just can't help as quickly and conveniently.

▲ **Avis** has a nationwide toll-free hotline (800-345-2847) that will send any distress call automatically to the nearest Avis outlet providing road service. Some of their phone systems let you know the closest 24-hour location.

▲ **Budget** has phone numbers in the rental contract; you can also call the 24-hour reservations number with your problem.

▲ **Hertz** provides a nationwide toll-free number (800-654-5060) and claims to be able to have renters back on the road in less than an hour in most cases. Alternatively, they send renters to appointments by taxi or other transport.

▲ **National** has an agreement with the Cross Country Motor Club, which has 15,000 service and towing affiliates and 24-hour service. Call 800-367-6767 for help. This service will also change flats and boost low batteries.

▲ **Dollar** has a similar arrangement with the Cross Country Motor Club. Their number is 800-235-9393.

▲ **Alamo** renters should call the central reservations number (800-327-9633). Alamo will dispatch a replacement car or authorize a repair.

International car-rental considerations

Driving or renting cars outside of the United States means dealing with an entirely different set of rules and laws. The law changes whether you pick up your car abroad or drive from the U.S. to Canada or Mexico.

International credit-card collision damage insurance

❏ If you use credit card CDW overseas, it is automatically considered primary coverage.

❏ Special conditions exist in some countries, specifically New Zealand and Italy, which require you to purchase local insurance regardless of credit card coverage. In New Zealand you must also put down a deposit on the automobile.

❏ Some foreign automobile rental agencies (and a few in the U.S.) may place a hold on a certain amount of your card credit. In some cases this may push the card over your credit limit.

❏ Credit holds are most common in the Caribbean and South America. Make sure to ask the car-rental reservationist whether a hold or deposit will be required. But beware: even if you get everything in writing here in the U.S., it may be worthless overseas. So plan on having to leave a deposit.

> ✔ NOTE: One solution to credit-card holds is to travel with two credit cards.

❏ If you are not using a credit card be aware that almost all U.S. automobile insurance policies are not in effect when driving outside the U.S. or Canada. Personal automobile insurance rarely provides coverage in foreign countries, owing to the variety of international insurance regulations and standards.

✦ AUTOMOBILE FACT ✦

The world's worst driver was reported in McKinney, Texas. A 75-year-old male driver received ten traffic tickets, drove on the wrong side of the road four times, committed four hit-and-run offenses and caused six accidents, all within 20 minutes on October 15, 1966.

International Driver's Permit

Though Canada and most countries in Europe recognize a U.S. driver's license, several such as Italy, Austria and Germany require local translations of the documents. For all other countries your best bet is to get an International Driving Permit from AAA.

International Driving Permits are good for a year. By mail, start the process a month before your departure. If you live near an AAA office, you can accomplish the entire process, including photos, there in less than a hour. International Driving Permits cost $10. Call (800) AAA-HELP for the forms and the location of the nearest office issuing permits. In Canada call (800) 336-HELP. You'll need:

- ❏ your license
- ❏ two passport-type photos, color or black and white (those from a dime-store photo booth are fine). If you have photos taken at a AAA office the cost is $8 for members, $10 for non-members.

✔ China, Egypt and Nepal do not permit foreigners to drive, and all rental cars come with chauffeurs.

Rules for driving to Canada and Mexico

Driving a rental car or your own car to Mexico or Canada requires a bit of preparation, especially if you are heading down Mexico way.

Canada:

❑ You need a U.S. driver's license, and remember to carry your passport or birth certificate to get back to the U.S.

❑ You must have a minimum amount of liability insurance equivalent to Cdn$200,000 (about US$160,000) everywhere except in the province of Quebec where the minimum is only Cdn$50,000 (about US$40,000).

❑ Most U.S. insurers cover drivers in Canada, but you should make sure. Though insurance cards are rarely asked for, have your insurance company send you a **Canadian Non-Resident Inter-Provincial Motor Vehicle Liability Insurance Card.**

Mexico:

❑ **Get ready for red tape.** And check before you go—everything will probably change with the implementation of NAFTA. For the time being, you will need a passport or certified copy of your birth certificate,

TRAVEL RIGHTS

valid U.S. driver's license, and Mexican Tourist Card if you plan to stay longer than three days.

❑ If you are taking your own car further than the immediate border area (loosely defined as within 10 to 12 miles of any border crossing) you'll need to take the original of your title or registration plus a copy. Then when you hit the border station for cars, about 12 miles inside the Mexican border, you can get your driving permit by paying $10 with a credit card issued by a bank outside Mexico. If you are driving a company car or a friend's car bring along a notarized letter authorizing you to drive the car, signed by the proper owner or the owner's representative.

❑ A new AAA program available in border states issues all immigration and customs forms. Fees vary.

❑ No matter how long you are staying be aware that your stateside insurance is probably no good in Mexico. You'll have to buy Mexican liability insurance from an office at the border crossing, from AAA or from the rental agency if you take a rental car. Credit-card collision insurance is good in Mexico.

❏ This routine is the same with rental car or personal auto. If you rent in Mexico you pay a very stiff price but eliminate much of the hassle.

> **NOTE:** Most rental agencies in San Diego, CA and San Antonio, TX as well as most major agencies near the Mexican border do not allow you to take their rental cars into Mexico.

Swiss highway tax

Tolls on superhighways in Switzerland are assessed as an annual road tax. If you don't want to drive on a superhighway, you don't pay the tax. However, for most of us traveling through Switzerland on vacation or business the superhighways are vital moving through the country quickly.

When the calendar-year toll is paid, a Swiss Autobahn decal is attached to the window of the car. Most rental cars in Europe have this toll paid. But if you are picking up a car at one end of Europe and driving through Switzerland, check to see whether the highway toll decal is in the window. If you arrive in Switzerland without the decal you will have to pay about $25 for one. Most rental companies will reimburse you for the cost, but if you don't know about this rule it can be a pain.

Renting cars in Eastern Europe

If you are planning a trip to Eastern Europe—Poland, The Czech Republic, The Slovak Republic, Hungary, Bulgaria or Romania—you may have to finesse your automobile rental because of the high rates of theft and vandalism.

This area of the world is changing rapidly and the economies are stabilizing. Experts feel that most of the current restrictions noted below will soon be lifted. Check with your rental agency or travel agency for the current rules and regulations when you make your arrangements.

Hertz, according to the *Consumer Reports Travel Letter*, makes the least restrictions on travel through Eastern Europe.

All other car rental companies have restrictions that vary from company to company and from country to country. For example:

- ❏ One company allows only cars rented in Switzerland to be taken into Eastern Europe.

- ❏ One limits East-West travel with rental cars to Austria and Hungary; another limits rentals to trips between Austria, Hungary and the Czech Republic.

- ❏ Many companies require you to purchase their own CDW.

- ❏ Several large European rental agencies won't allow any cars to cross into Eastern Europe.

- ❏ The French and Belgians offer automobile *leases*, which have no restrictions.

> According to the credit card companies their collision damage insurance is good throughout Eastern Europe, but finding a rental company who will accept the insurance can be difficult.

✔ **NOTE:** Unleaded gas is next to impossible to find. If you are planning a trip into Eastern Europe, rent a car that takes normal leaded gas. Eastern Germany has plenty of unleaded gas pumps and Hungary has a respectable number, but they are hard to find.

CREDIT CARD
BENEFITS

Travelers should carefully look into the benefits of their credit cards. MasterCard, Visa and Discover are credit and charge cards that allow payments for travel and purchases over a period of time. American Express and Diners Club are travel and entertainment cards that require full payment of your balance each month except in the case of airline tickets, which may be paid for over several months with American Express.

Credit cards can be used either to obtain credit and stretch the payment period or as a travel tool to allow additional flexibility and consumer protection. In the first case, just looking for the card with the lowest interest rate and annual fee is the governing factor. However, when looking at a credit card as a travel tool, everything requires a different focus. This chapter outline some of what different credit and charge cards offer travelers. There is no way to cover *all* the fine print here. We hope only to provide a look at the most important considerations.

As noted in the Auto Rights chapter, many corporate and individual credit cartds provide collision damage insurance. American Express, Diners Club, Discover, Visa and MasterCard also provide an array of wide-ranging and quite valuable insurance coverages. Not much has been made of this by the travel media. The conventional wisdom is that these coverages merely duplicate what you already have. But conventional wisdom can be very short-sighted, especially when some of the benefits of gold cards and business cards are taken into account.

The list of additional coverages provided by various cards is impressive, and all are in effect worldwide unless specifically limited. The basic benefits that are most important to travelers are shown below. These coverages vary card by card and bank by bank so read your cardmember agreement carefully.

Abbreviations used in this section:
   AX=American Express
   DC=Diners Club
   D=Discover.
   MC=standard MasterCard
   GMC=Gold MasterCard
   MCBC=MasterCard BusinessCard
   V=standard Visa
   VG=Visa Gold

● **Buyer protection benefit**
  (V, VG, MC, GMC, AX, D)

This is offered by virtually every card to U.S. (the 50 states, D.C., Puerto Rico, and U.S. Virgin Islands) cardholders. It protects any purchases made with your card against damage and theft for (normally) 90 days from date of purchase. This protection is limited to $1,000 per occurrence for most cards with a variable monetary limit per card (normally about $50,000).

> This is often secondary insurance which pays after you have already been indemnified by your homeowner, auto or renter's insurance. It is excellent for covering deductibles.

✔ **TRAVELER'S NOTE:** Items stolen from a car, whether left in the car or part of the automobile equipment, are not covered. Items stolen or damaged in checked baggage are not covered. Hand baggage is covered. Gifts purchased with the card that you give to others are also covered. Confiscation by customs officials is not covered nor are Acts of God, war or hostilities of any kind.

> **NOTE:** Stolen items *must* be reported to the police or an appropriate authority within 36 to 45 hours. Failure to get a police report will negate any coverage.

- **Automatic travel accident insurance**
  (V, VG, MC, GMC, MCBC, AX, DC, D)

This coverage is relatively gruesome dealing with death and dismemberment. The only point here is to be aware that you (or another who may have charged tickets) may have additional insurance for injury or death while traveling on any public carrier be it train, plane, ship, airport shuttle, or other transport from the time of leaving home for the airport or terminal until returning home. The amount of coverage depends on the type of card you have. Some examples—AT&T Universal standard cards provide $100,000; the AT&T Universal Gold MasterCard and AT&T Universal Visa Gold provide $250,000; and Discover offers $500,000 of insurance.

> ☆ The best coverage with this type of insurance is Diners Club, which not only provides $350,000 of life insurance if travelers purchased their tickets with their Diners Club credit card, but also offers coverage for current Diners Club members traveling on free tickets such as frequent flier awards.

Travel assistance services

You can call a toll-free number provided by your credit card and receive information that will help you plan your trip and help if things go wrong *during* your trip. These benefits can be real time-savers, and the money transfer features save you money. Perhaps the best part of these services is that the card travel service center can serve almost as a secretary and message center in an emergency. This includes:

✦ information on passport and visa requirements, immunizations, currency exchange rates and weather forecasts.

✦ arranging to transfer up to $5,000 from a family member, friend or business.

✦ assisting in replacement of important documents including lost passports and tickets. You are responsible for the cost of replacements.

✦ Help in locating luggage if it is lost by a common carrier. Transport of luggage to your location is at your expense.

✔ **NOTE:** If you have a Gold MasterCard, Visa Gold, American Express, Diners Club, or MasterCard BusinessCard and you travel more than 50 or 100 miles away from your home (depending on the card) additional travel assistance programs take effect generally as follows (specifics vary depending on the card):

● **Worldwide legal referral assistance**
(VG, GMC, MCBC, AX, DC)
Referrals to English-speaking attorneys and contact with U.S. embassies and consulates will be arranged in case of arrest, an automobile accident or need of other legal assistance. In addition most credit card companies can assist in transferring bail payments from your personal accounts or your credit card credit line. The assistance centers normally follow up to insure that the bail is handled properly.

● **Emergency message services**
(VG, GMC, MCBC, AX, DC)
Credit card assistance centers will pass along emergency messages to friends, family and business associates. This allows you to make only one call to the assistance center. They do the rest.

● **Emergency transportation and**
medical assistance
(VG, GMC, MCBC, AX, DC)
If you become ill during a trip, most credit card assistance centers will help make arrangements to bring you home or transfer

TRAVEL
RIGHTS

you to another hospital. These assistance centers will all arrange to get children home and provide a continuing contact with family members. In the event of death, these travel assistance programs help with the transfer of remains back home. They will also assist in making travel arrangements to bring a family member or close friend to your bedside if you are traveling alone and have a travel emergency. All expenses are paid for by the cardmember or the cardmember's estate.

Both Visa and MasterCard Gold cards will assist in filling prescriptions.
If the prescriptions are not locally available, they will arrange for delivery.

☆ MasterCardBusinessCard goes several big steps further than just assistance with their unique MasterAssist/Medical program. These benefits are available to card holders regardless of what method was used to pay for the trip. *(These specific benefits only apply to MasterCard BusinessCards, not any other type of MasterCard)*

• This credit card will actually pay for any transfers necessary due to an accident or sudden illness while traveling more than 100 miles away from home (with the exception of about a dozen countries). This coverage also extends to spouses and unmarried dependent children.

• You are covered for $2,500 of medical expenses for such occurrences with only $50 deductible per person.

• If hospitalization is expected to last eight days or longer, and you are traveling with dependent children, MasterAssist will arrange and pay for their safe return home.

• If you are traveling alone and will be hospitalized outside the U.S. for more than eight days, MasterAssist staff can arrange and pay for an economy class round-trip ticket to bring one relative or friend to your bedside.

• In the event of the death of an immediate relative while traveling outside the 50 United States, they will arrange and pay for a cardholder's return trip to the U.S.

• In the unfortunate event of the death of a cardmember or covered family while traveling, MasterAssist will make all necessary arrangements and pay for shipment home of the remains of the deceased.

● **Emergency translation services**
(VG, GMC, MCBC, AX, DC)
Provide free telephone translation services and will help secure a local interpreter at your expense if more assistance is needed.

● Lost luggage coverage
(American Express and Diners Club)

• With American Express Platinum you are covered for up to $1,250 for carry-on baggage and up to $500 over and above the coverage provided by the common carrier for checked baggage. With the normal American Express card you are covered for reimbursement for up to $200 for delayed bags and up to $500 in excess of the airline's liability if your checked or carry-on bags are lost or damaged. American Express coverage is for *original* cost.

• With Diners Club you are covered for $1,250 above and beyond the carrier's indemnity. This coverage is based on *replacement* value of items.

● Valuable document delivery

If you forget a critical document, the cardmember assistance center can arrange to pick up and deliver the document to you.

● Frequent flier mileage

Many credit cards now give frequent flier mileage, based on your overall spending. Nearly every airline has a Visa or Master-Card affinity card, which gives you mileage with them, so you'll have to decide which airline you want to collect mileage on, and apply for that affinity card. The amount of mileage you can get is usually subject to a monthly limit.

American Express *Membership Miles* offers points on less than a half-dozen airlines, for an extra fee with most of their cards. You must spend $5,000 during a given 12-month period, and mileage only carries over if you reach the $5,000 threshold again during the next 12-month period.

Diners Club *Club Rewards* offers mileage on practically every major airline, with no extra fee and no annual purchase minimums. You can transfer mileage to any participating program. It is by far the best of the credit card frequent flier deals.

AUTHOR'S CREDIT CARD RECOMMENDATIONS

These recommendations are based strictly on the travel benefits offered by the cards.

☆ Choose Diners Club if you are a frequent traveler for either business or pleasure.
  • Their CDW insurance is the best.
  • Club Rewards is the best credit card frequent flier mileage program
  • The baggage insurance is based on replacement costs (limited to $1,250).
  • The common carrier life insurance is the best available with credit cards and covers free travel such as frequent flier travel.

☆ Choose MasterCard BusinessCard for medical coverage. These benefits far surpass anything offered by other cards.

TAX RIGHTS

One class of rights nearly all travelers have, but don't know much about, concerns taxes, notably sales taxes here in the United States and Value Added Taxes (VATs) in many other countries.

The pleasant fact is that in many cases you don't have to pay these taxes or can get your money back, after you pay them with your purchase at the store, when you leave the country.

> ✔ These tax avoidance actions can save you as much as 20 percent on some purchases in Europe, 7 to 19 percent in Canada, and up to 8.5 percent here in the U.S.

United States

In the U.S. when you are making a large purchase in a state with a hefty sales tax (one greater than the sales tax in your home state), you may ask the store to ship the item to your home. This way you may avoid sales taxes altogether, or at least be charged the lower tax rate of the state to which the merchandise has been sent. This procedure can also help trim your luggage weight but let you enjoy all your souvenirs when you get home.

Canada

In Canada, there is a national Goods and Services Tax (GST), similar to VAT, of 7 percent. Plus, in all Canadian provinces except Alberta, the Northwest Territories, and the Yukon, an additional Provincial Sales Tax (PST) levied.

■ **Refunds of GST** can be claimed for taxes paid on items taken out of Canada within 60 days of purchase. You can also get GST refunds for hotel rooms. The list of items which do *not* allow GST refunds includes gasoline, tobacco, alcoholic beverages, meals, car rentals and camping fees.

To file for a refund of GST you must fill out GST refund forms available in most hotels and many stores. These forms are then returned to Canada with *originals* of all receipts upon which you are requesting credit. The minimum refund is Cdn$7 and if your claim is less than Cdn$500 a day you may make your claim at the border. In any case all claims must be made within one year of any purchase involved in the claim.

This is not a speedy process. At the border or airport, expect at least 15 minutes of paperwork even if you have all your *original* receipts together. It is not difficult to calculate the time required based on observation of the people in line in front of you .

NOTE: If you process your GST claims by mail, the government will return your receipts with your refund. If you are also claiming a refund for PST taxes, send the request in after you complete the GST portion of the refund—the provinces do not normally return the receipts.

CANADIAN PROVINCIAL SALES TAXES

\$\$ In British Columbia the PST is 6 percent; in Saskatchewan, 7 percent; and in Prince Edward Island, 10 percent. These provinces treat PST as U.S. states treat sales taxes—they can only be eliminated from items being sent out of province.

\$\$ In Quebec refunds of the 8 percent PST are only authorized for purchases of more than Cdn\$500.

\$\$ Ontario PST is 8 percent with a minimum claim of Cdn\$7.

\$\$ Nova Scotia PST is 10 percent with a minimum claim of Cdn\$16.

\$\$ New Brunswick PST is 11 percent.

\$\$ Newfoundland PST is 12 percent with a minimum claim of Cdn\$12.

\$\$ Manitoba PST is currently 7 percent.

■ **PST refunds** are not permitted on meals or automobile rentals. Refunds must be requested from each province separately and each has a different procedure for requesting them. The refund forms may be obtained at many stores, hotels and visitor centers. As with GST, PST refunds require receipts with taxes clearly noted, and proof that the items have been exported, but the PST refund request must be received in the provincial offices within 30 days of the purchase.

Europe

Value Added Taxes (VAT) in Europe are a way of life. Virtually everything you purchase, from a *Wurst* or *café* on the street to the latest fashions in trendy boutiques, has VAT included somewhere. It is always clearly marked on your bill or receipt if you ask for one.

These VATs are not chicken feed. They run up to 20 percent in some countries, and vary depending on what you purchase: luxury goods are saddled with a higher tax than necessities.

Theoretically, anyone taking any goods out of a country could be reimbursed the VAT paid on items purchased there, but it was much easier to explain and legislate the theory than it is to actually accomplish the task.

VAT refund counters at airports stamp receipts, approve refund claim forms, and provide envelopes to send VAT refund claims back to the stores from which items were purchased. However, these systems are slow, slow, slow. In addition, you'll have to return forms to *each* store in which you made purchases.

Maximum VATs in Europe	
Austria	16.7%
Belgium	16.3%
Denmark	20.0%
Finland	18.0%
France	15.7%
Germany	13.0%
Greece	15.3%
Italy	16.0%
Luxembourg	13.0%
Netherlands	14.9%
Norway	18.0%
Portugal	13.8%
Spain	13.0%
Sweden	20.0%
U.K.	14.9%

A simplified VAT refund program has recently been started in Europe and includes at least the 15 countries listed in the table above. This new program is called Europe Tax-free Shopping (ETS) and organizers expect it to continue to expand. Basically, ETS does all the paperwork for you for a 20 percent commission. Here's how it works:

- Look for a store displaying the ETS shopping logo. Over 60,000 stores and boutiques, and Europe's largest department stores, participate.

- When you make your purchase, ask the salesperson to fill out a VAT-refund check. There is a minimum purchase requirement, ranging from about $13 to over $350, which varies by country. This refund check reflects the VAT you paid, with the 20 percent service charge deducted. When you leave the country, you get the check stamped by customs officials and then cash it at one of 3,000 windows at most airports and border crossings. Some of these windows will even convert your funds to U.S. dollars, and others will transfer credit to your credit card.

- For information on this system write: European Tax-Free Shopping, P.O. Box 9012, East Setauket, NY 11733.

CONSULAR SERVICES

WHAT CAN THEY DO FOR YOU?

There are two sections of consular services from which Americans traveling abroad may need assistance—the Passport Office and the Citizen Services Office.

The Passport Office handles the issuing of new passports (see next page). The Citizen Services Office handles about everything else. Rather than solving problems, they attempt to provide travelers with enough information to help themselves.

◆ They maintain lists of English-speaking lawyers and doctors. They may know one specializing in your problem or illness.

◆ U.S. officials are usually notified within 48 hours if you are arrested. They will visit, explain the justice system, check on conditions, and help contact your family.

◆ Consulates can quickly transfer emergency funds through the Citizen Services Trust Fund. However, they do not in general pay expenses or lend money.

✔ NOTE: The consulate or embassy is not a bank—it can't cash checks or make loans; it is not a travel agency—it can't make hotel reservations or flight arrangements, or recommend sights.

What to do if your passport is lost

✔ About 27,000 U.S. passports are lost or stolen abroad every year.

❑ Report the loss immediately to the local authorities.

❑ Contact the closest U.S. embassy or consulate. There is always a duty officer on call who can usually get you a replacement or obtain permission for you to return to the States.

❑ If you have lost all your identification, bring along anyone who can vouch for your citizenship, or anything that might prove your identity (plane tickets, engraved jewelry, a prescription bottle, or the like).

❑ Do not go to the airport and expect to be allowed to board a plane back to the United States. This won't work and you're wasting precious time.

❑ Make two copies of all travel documents and identification papers before you leave—e.g., tickets, driver's license, passport. Take one copy (keep it separate from your passport) and leave one with someone back home whom you can call in an emergency.

❑ If you find your passport after you've already applied for a new one, return the old one to the passport-issuing office.

❑ If you received a limited/emergency passport abroad, upon arrival home, take it to a passport agency with proof of citizenship, identification and explanation of loss. They will issue a new permanent passport.

from *Travel Holiday*, compiled with assistance from the U.S. State Department

TRAVEL RIGHTS

EFFECTIVE
COMPLAINING

When passengers comment on airline service, most airlines do listen. They analyze and keep track of the complaints and compliments they receive and use the information to determine what the public wants and to identify problem areas that need special attention. They also try to resolve individual complaints.

Like other businesses, airlines have a lot of discretion in how they respond to problems. Within your legal rights, your demands for monetary compensation will probably be subject to negotiation, and the kind of action you get depends in large part on the way you go about complaining.

Start with the airline. Before you call or write the DOT or some other agency for help with an air travel problem, you should give the airline a chance to resolve it. Uncle Sam usually doesn't get involved in consumer disputes that go beyond luggage, overbooking, delays and cancellations on domestic flights.

Consumer Reports Travel Letter notes a phenomenon called Merkel's Law (supposedly named after a veteran ticket agent): *A passenger no longer standing in front of you is no longer a problem.* Daily, this law comes into play unless you push the customer service representative into a corner. Ask if an on-the-spot rule waiver might solve the problem.

As a rule, airlines have trouble-shooters at the airports (they're usually called Customer Service Representatives) who can take care of most problems on the spot, and do a lot to make your problems easier to deal with. They can:

- arrange meals and hotel rooms for stranded passengers
- write checks for denied boarding compensation
- endorse tickets to other carriers
- arrange for luggage repairs
- send delayed luggage to your home
- provide taxi vouchers to hotels or between airports
- provide meal and drink vouchers
- settle other routine claims or complaints that involve relatively small amounts of money.

If you can't resolve the problem at the airport and want to file a complaint, it's best to call or write the airline's consumer office or customer relations. Take notes at the time the incident occurs and jot down the names of the airline employees with whom you dealt. Keep all your travel documents (ticket receipts, baggage check stubs, boarding passes, etc.) as well as receipts for any out-of-pocket expenses that were incurred as a result of the mishandling. Here are some helpful letter-writing tips.

- Type the letter and, if at all possible, limit it to one page.

- Include a daytime telephone number where you can be reached.

- No matter how angry you may be, keep your letter businesslike in tone and don't exaggerate what happened. If the complaint sounds very vehement or sarcastic when you read it back, you might consider waiting a day and rewriting it.

- Start by saying what reservations you held, what happened and at which ticket office, airport or flight the incident occurred.

- Send copies, never the originals, of tickets, receipts or other documents that can back up your claim.

- Include the names of any employees who were rude or made things worse, as well as especially helpful employees.

- Don't clutter up your complaint with petty gripes that can obscure what you're really angry about.

- Let the airline know if you've suffered any special inconvenience or monetary loss.

- Say just what you expect the carrier to do to make amends. An airline may offer to settle your claim with a check or some other kind of compensation, possibly free transportation. You may only want a written apology from a rude employee—but the airline needs to know what you want before it can decide what action to take.

- Be reasonable. If your demands are way out of line, your letter could earn you a polite apology and a place in the airline's crank files.

If you follow these guidelines, the airlines will probably treat your complaint seriously. Your letter will help them to determine what caused your problem, as well as to suggest actions the company can take to keep the same thing from happening to other people.

CONTACTING THE DEPARTMENT OF TRANSPORTATION AND FAA

If you need assistance or want to put your complaint about an airline on record with the DOT, call the Office of Consumer Affairs at ☎ 202-366-2220 Monday through Friday from 8:15 a.m. to 4:45 p.m. Eastern Standard Time or write:

Office of Consumer Affairs
U.S. Department of Transportation
400 7th Street, S.W. Room 10405
Washington, D.C. 20590

If you choose to write, please be sure to include your name, return address and daytime telephone number. A photocopy of your airline ticket may also help.

The DOT will frequently contact the airline to determine if your complaint was properly handled and get back to you. They also provide information about what rights you may or may not have under Federal laws.

Letters from consumers help DOT spot problem areas and trends in the airline industry. Every month they publish a report with information about the number of complaints they receive about each airline and what problems people are having. They also use DOT complaint files to document the need for changes in the DOT's consumer protection regulations.

If your complaint is about something you feel is a safety hazard, call or write to the Federal Aviation Administration:

Community & Consumer Liaison Divison
APA-200
Federal Aviation Administration
800 Independence Avenue, S.W.
Washington, D.C. 20591
Toll-free ☎ 800-FAA-SURE
Office hours: Monday - Friday 8 a.m. to 4 p.m. Eastern Standard Time

Safety issues include carry-on baggage, child safety seats, airport security procedures, aircraft malfunctions, air traffic systems, and hazardous materials.

The U.S. Government Printing Office offers books and pamphlets covering many of your travel rights including *Fly Rights,* which is incorporated in this book, *Child/Infant Safety Seats Recommended for Use in Aircraft,* and *Your Trip Abroad.* Write for the free Consumer Information Catalog, P.O. Box 100, Pueblo, CO 81002.

TRAVEL INDUSTRY CONSUMER PROTECTION PROGRAMS

These two organizations provide good industry-based consumer affairs programs:

American Society of Travel Agents (ASTA)
1101 King Street
Alexandria, VA 22314
☎ 703-739-2782

United States Tour Operator Association
211 E. 51st Street, #12B
New York, NY 10022
☎ 212-944-5727

ASTA may be able to help if your complaint is against a member travel agent or one of the travel suppliers booked *through* a travel agency. You must submit complaints to ASTA within six months of the incident.

The United States Tour Operator Association represents about 40 large wholesale tour operators. Their assistance programs are very helpful when member organizations are involved.

LOCAL CONSUMER
HELP PROGRAMS

In most communities there are consumer help groups that try to mediate complaints about businesses, including airlines and travel agencies.

- Most state governments have a special office that investigates consumer problems and complaints. Sometimes it is a separate division in the governor's or state attorney general's office. Check your telephone book under the state government listing.

- Many cities and counties have consumer affairs departments that handle complaints. Often you can register your complaint and get information over the phone or in person.

- Your local Better Business Bureau can often help resolve disputes.

- A number of newspapers and radio or TV stations operate Hot Lines or Action Lines where individual consumers can get help. Consumer reporters, with the help of volunteers, try to mediate complaints and may report the results as a news item. The possible publicity encourages companies to take fast action on consumer problems when they are referred by the media. Some Action Lines, however, may not be able to handle every complaint they receive. They often select the most severe problems or those that are most representative of the kinds of complaints they get.

● *Condé Nast TRAVELER* has sections called Ombudsman and Question & Answer that provide help in settling some travel-related problems. However, their problem solving and answers are limited to those problems they discuss in the magazine. The address and fax numbers for these sections are published monthly in the magazine.

● *Travel Holiday* includes excellent information for travelers in their Travel Advisor section.

● There are also several good books which can be found in libraries covering travel rules and regulations.

AIRLINE CUSTOMER

SERVICE CONTACTS

Air Wisconsin
Consumer Affairs
Administrator
203 Challenger Drive
Appleton, WI 54915
☎800-424-9050

Alaska Airlines
Director
Consumer Affairs
PO Box 68900
Seattle, WA 98168
☎206-431-7286

Aloha Airlines
Manager
Customer Relations
PO Box 30028
Honolulu, HI 96820
☎808-836-4115

America West Airlines
Manager
Customer Relations
4000 E. Sky Harbor
Blvd.
Phoenix, AZ 85034
☎800-235-9292
ext. 6019

American Airlines
Director
Consumer Relations
PO Box 619612
M/D 2400
Dallas/Ft. Worth
Airport
Ft. Worth, TX 75261
☎817-967-2000

American Trans Air
Consumer Affairs
PO Box 51609,
Indianapolis
International Airport
Indianapolis, IN
46251
☎317-243-4140

Continental Airlines
Director
Customer Relations
3663 Sam Houston
Parkway, E. #500
Houston, TX 77032
☎713-987-6500

Delta Airlines, Inc.
Director
Consumer Affairs
Hartsfield-Atlanta
Airport
Atlanta, GA 30320
☎404-715-1450

Hawaiian Airlines
Manager
Consumer Affairs
PO Box 30008
Honolulu, HI 96820
☎808-835-3424

Horizon Air
Manager
Customer Relations
PO Box 48309
Seattle, WA 98148
☎800-523-1223
ext. 601

Markair, Inc.
Customer Affairs
Representative
PO Box 196769
4100 International
Airport
Anchorage, AK
99519
☎800-544-0181

**Midwest Express
Airlines, Inc.**
Consumer Affairs
Specialist
4915 S. Howel
Avenue
Milwaukee, WI
53207
☎414-747-4000

Northwest Airlines
Director
Customer Relations
5101 Northwest Drive
St. Paul, MN 55111
☎612-726-2046

Southwest Airlines
Director
Customer Relations
PO Box 36611
Love Field
Dallas, TX 75235
☎214-904-4223

Tower Air, Inc.
Manager
Customer Service
Hangar No. 17
JFK Int'l Airport
Jamaica, NY 11430
☎718-553-4300

Trans World Airlines
Staff VP
Customer Relations
110 S. Bedford Road
Mt. Kisco, NY 10549
☎914-242-3172

United Airlines
Director
Customer Relations
PO Box 66100
Chicago, IL 60666
☎708-952-6796

**USAir
USAir Shuttle**
Director
Consumer Affairs
PO Box 1501
Winston-Salem, NC
27102
☎703-892-7020
or 919-661-0061

Westair Airlines
VP Customer Service
5570 Air Terminal Dr.
Fresno, CA 93727
☎209-294-6915

These are the major
and national U.S.
airlines, ranked in the
DOT's monthly report
of service complaints.

Car rental customer
Service contacts

Avis
Customer Service
900 Old Country Rd.
Garden City, NY
11530
☎800-352-7900 or
516-222-4200

Alamo
Customer Relations
PO Box 22776
Ft. Lauderdale, FL
33335
☎800-445-5664

Budget
Customer Relations
PO Box 111520
Carrollton, TX 75011
☎800-621-2844

Dollar
Consumer Services
100 N. Sepulveda
Blvd., 6th floor
El Segundo, CA
90245
☎800-800-5252

Hertz
Customer Relations
PO Box 26120
Oklahoma City, OK
73126
☎800-654-4173

National
VP, Customer Service
and Quality
7700 France Ave. S.
Minneapolis, MN
55435
☎800-367-6767 or
612-830-2951

Thrifty
Customer Service
PO Box 35250
Tulsa, OK 74135
☎800-334-1705

Value
Customer Service
PO Box 5040
Boca Raton, FL 33431
☎800-327-6459

CREDIT CARD CONTACTS

American Express
Green ☎800-528-4800
Gold ☎800-327-2177
Plat'm ☎800-525-3355

Diners Club
☎800-2-DINERS
Discover Card
☎800-DISCOVER

Visa & MasterCard: These have different
benefits from bank to bank—call the phone
number on the back of your card.

TRAVEL
RIGHTS

INDEX

**TRAVEL
RIGHTS
146**

TRAVEL RIGHTS